# How to DeFi

*1st Edition, March 2020*

Darren Lau, Daryl Lau, Teh Sze Jin,
Kristian Kho, Erina Azmi,
TM Lee, Bobby Ong

"DeFi can be intimidating and overly complex, but this book makes it simple."

— Seb Audet, Founder of DeFiSnap

"If I didn't know anything about DeFi and needed to learn from scratch, this book is where I'd start."

— Felix Feng, CEO of TokenSets

"This book makes it easy for beginners to get started with DeFi."

— Hugh Karp, CEO of Nexus Mutual

"There is a lot of content about decentralized finance available but nothing matches this depth and comprehensiveness of this book."

— Leighton Cusack, CEO of PoolTogether

"This is an excellent resource for anyone who wants a comprehensive introduction to DeFi."

— Kain Warwick, Founder of Synthetix

"This book details the new economies created by a generation of bankless pioneers. It's the best introduction you could ask for."

— Mariano Conti, Head of Smart Contracts at Maker Foundation

# CONTENTS

What is a Dashboard?
DeFiSnap: Step-by-Step Guide

## Part Four: DeFi in Action

## Chapter 14: DeFi in Action
Surviving Argentina's High Inflation
Uniswap Ban

## Chapter 15: DeFi is the Future, and the Future is Now
What about DeFi User Experience?

## Closing Remarks

## Appendix
CoinGecko's Recommended DeFi Resources
Information
Newsletters
Podcast
Youtube
Bankless Level-Up Guide
Projects We Like Too
Dashboard Interfaces
Decentralized Exchanges
Exchange Aggregators
Lending and Borrowing
Prediction Markets
Taxes
Wallet
Yield Optimisers
References
Chapter 1: Traditional Financial Institutions
Chapter 2: What is Decentralized Finance (DeFi)?
Chapter 3: The Decentralized Layer: Ethereum
Chapter 4: Ethereum Wallets
Chapter 5: Decentralized Stablecoins
Chapter 6: Decentralized Borrowing and Lending
Chapter 7: Decentralized Exchange (DEX)
Chapter 8: Decentralized Derivatives
Chapter 9: Decentralized Fund Management
Chapter 10: Decentralized Lottery
Chapter 11: Decentralized Payment
Chapter 12: Decentralized Insurance
Chapter 13: Dashboard
Chapter 14: DeFi in Action

## Glossary

# INTRODUCTION

Welcome to CoinGecko's very first book, **How to DeFi**! DeFi is the acronym for the term Decentralized Finance and is currently one of the fastest-growing sectors in the blockchain and cryptocurrency space. DeFi has grown very rapidly in the past one year but materials to help people grasp the idea of DeFi lagged behind. We set out on our research in this exciting new space and condensed all of our findings into the 1st Edition of this book here.

DeFi is an ecosystem of Decentralized Applications (Dapps) that provide financial services built on top of distributed networks with no governing authority. A majority of the DeFi Dapps currently being built are on the Ethereum blockchain, so for purposes of brevity, this will be the focus in this book.

DeFi has been the key theme in Ethereum's development in 2019 and 2020. At this point of writing, DeFi Dapps have locked up over $1 billion worth of cryptocurrencies. DeFi is expected to grow further in the coming years and is a key component in fulfilling Ethereum's lofty vision and ambition.

In this book, we will be explaining what DeFi is and how it is important for the community. We will be looking at the various elements of DeFi such as decentralized stablecoins, decentralized exchanges, decentralized lending, decentralized derivatives, and decentralized insurance. In each of these chapters, we will be providing step-by-step guides to assist you to interact with at least one of the DeFi products.

1

Throughout the book, we will have **Recommended Readings** at the end of each chapter. In these sections, we will share supplementary reading materials that we believe will be useful as you dive deeper into the DeFi ecosystem - all credits of course go to their respective authors. Kudos to them for making DeFi more accessible!

This book is aimed at DeFi beginners so if you are a DeFi expert, do kindly share with us how we can further improve it to make DeFi friendlier for other beginners in our future editions. To accelerate the DeFi adoption, we want to make the complex designs of DeFi simple for the public to understand and accessible for them to get started.

We hope that by sharing our learnings with you, we will help you get up to speed with DeFi and are able to join us to participate in this movement.

**CoinGecko Research Team**
Darren Lau, Daryl Lau, Teh Sze Jin, Kristian Kho, Erina Azmi, TM Lee, Bobby Ong
20 February 2020

# PART ONE: CENTRALIZED & DECENTRALIZED FINANCE

# CHAPTER 1: THE TRADITIONAL FINANCIAL INSTITUTIONS

In our attempt to shed light on people new to DeFi, we'll start by first going through the basics of how traditional financial institutions work. For simplicity, we will focus on the highest leveraged institutions in the traditional financial system, the banks, and discuss its key areas to see the potential risks.

## The Banks

Banks are the giants of the financial industry that facilitate payments, accept deposits and offer lines of credit to individuals, businesses, other financial institutions, and even governments. In fact, they are so large that the total market capitalization of the top 10 banks in the world is valued at $2 trillion USD. In contrast, the total market capitalization of the **entire** cryptocurrency market was valued at approximately $200 billion on the 31st of December 2019.

| Top 10 Global Banks 2019 | | | |
|---|---|---|---|
| **Rank** | **Bank** | **Country** | **Market Cap. ($ bn)** |
| 1 | ICBC | China | 338 |
| 2 | China Construction Bank | China | 287 |
| 3 | Agricultural Bank of China | China | 243 |
| 4 | Bank of China | China | 230 |
| 5 | JP Morgan Chase | US | 209 |
| 6 | Bank of America | US | 189 |
| 7 | Wells Fargo | US | 168 |
| 8 | Citigroup | US | 158 |
| 9 | HSBC | UK | 147 |
| 10 | Mitsubishi UFJ | Japan | 146 |

*Source: Top 1000 World Banks 2019*

Banks are vital parts of the moving machine that is the financial industry—they enable money to move around the world by providing value transfer services (deposit, withdrawal, transfers), extend credit lines (loans), and more. However, banks are managed by humans and governed by policies that are prone to human-related risks such as mismanagement and corruption.

The global financial crisis of 2008 exemplified excessive risk-taking by banks and governments were forced to make massive bailouts of the banks. The crisis exposed the shortcomings of the traditional financial system and highlighted a need for it to be better.

DeFi seeks to build a better financial landscape made possible by the advent of the internet and blockchain technology, particularly in three key segments of the banking system:
1. Payment & clearance system (remittance)
2. Accessibility
3. Centralization & Transparency

1. **Payment and Clearance System**

If you've tried to send money to someone or a business in another country, you know this pain all too well—remittances involving banks worldwide typically take a few working days to complete[1] and involve all sorts of fees. To make matters worse, there may also be issues with documentation, compliance with anti-money laundering laws, privacy concerns, and more.

For example, if you are living in the US and would like to send USD $1,000 from your bank account in the US to your friend's bank account in Australia, there are typically three fees involved: the exchange rate from your bank, the international wire outbound fee and the international wire inbound fee. Additionally, it will take a few working days for the recipient to receive the money depending on the recipient bank's location.

Cryptocurrencies that powers the DeFi movement allow you to bypass intermediaries who take the lion's share of profits of these transfers. It is likely to be quicker as well - your transfers would be processed with no questions asked with relatively lower fees compared to banks. For example, the transfer of cryptocurrencies to any account in the world would take anywhere between 15 seconds to 5 minutes depending on several factors[2], along with a small fee (e.g. $0.02 on Ethereum).

2. **Accessibility**

Chances are if you are reading this book, you are banked and have access to financial services offered by banks—to open a savings account, take a loan, make investments and more. However, there are also many more who are less fortunate and do not have access to even the most basic savings account.

---

[1] "How Long Does It Take to Have a Payment Post Online to ...." 2 Jul. 2017, https://www.gobankingrates.com/banking/checking-account/how-long-payment-posted-online-account/.

[2] "How long does an Ethereum transaction really take? - ETH ...." 5 Jun. 2019, https://ethgasstation.info/blog/ethereum-transaction-how-long/.

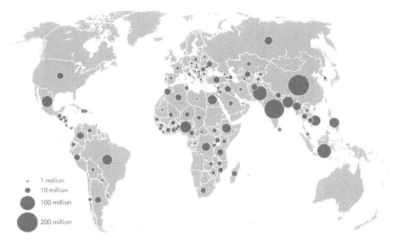

*Heatmap of the Unbanked (Source: Global Findex, World Bank, 2017)*

The World Bank estimates that as of 2017, there are 1.7 billion people who do not own an account at a financial institution and more than half of them are from developing nations[3]. They come largely from poor households and some of their main reasons for not having a bank account are due to poverty, geographical and trust issues.

For the 1.7 billion unbanked, access to banking is tough—but DeFi has the potential to make it easier. Accessing DeFi Dapps only requires a person to have a mobile phone & internet access, as opposed to going through lengthy verification processes. The World Bank estimates that two-thirds of the 1.7 billion unbanked have access to mobile phones[4] and DeFi Dapps can be their gateway to accessing financial products as opposed to traditional banks.

DeFi represents a movement that seeks to push borderless, censorship-free and accessible financial products for all. DeFi protocols do not discriminate and levels the playing field for everyone.

---

[3] "2 THE UNBANKED - Global Findex."
https://globalfindex.worldbank.org/sites/globalfindex/files/chapters/2017%20Findex%20full%20report_chapter2.pdf.

[4] "Insights from the World Bank's 2017 Global Findex database ...." 20 Apr. 2018, https://www.devex.com/news/insights-from-the-world-bank-s-2017-global-findex-database-92589.

## 3. Centralization & Transparency

There is no denying that traditional, regulated financial institutions that comply with government laws and regulations such as banks are some of the most secure places to park funds. But they are not without flaws—even large banks can fail. Washington Mutual with over $188 billion[5] in deposits and Lehman Brothers with $639 billion[6] in assets have both failed in 2008. In the US alone, over 500 bank failures have been recorded[7].

Banks are one of the centralized points of failure in the financial system—the fall of Lehman Brother triggered the start of the 2008 financial crisis. The centralization of power and funds in the hands of the banks is dangerous, and rightfully so looking at past incidents.

Transparency also ties into this - there is no way for regular investors to fully know what financial institutions do. Some of the events leading up to the 2008 financial crisis included credit rating agencies giving AAA ratings (best & safest investments) to high-risk mortgage-backed securities[8].

It will be different with DeFi. DeFi protocols built on top of public blockchains such as Ethereum are mostly open-sourced for audit and transparency purposes. They usually have decentralized governing organizations to ensure that everyone knows what is happening and that no bad actors can single-handedly make bad decisions.

DeFi protocols are written as lines of codes—you can't cheat the codes as it treats every participant equally without discrimination. The codes run exactly as they are programmed to, and any flaws quickly

---

[5] "Washington Mutual (WaMu): How It Went Bankrupt."
https://www.thebalance.com/washington-mutual-how-wamu-went-bankrupt-3305620.

[6] "The Collapse of Lehman Brothers: A Case ...." 26 Nov. 2019,
https://www.investopedia.com/articles/economics/09/lehman-brothers-collapse.asp.

[7] "Failed Bank List – FDIC."
https://www.fdic.gov/bank/individual/failed/banklist.html.

[8] "financial crisis – GovInfo." https://www.govinfo.gov/content/pkg/GPO-FCIC/pdf/GPO-FCIC.pdf.

become evident as it is open for public scrutiny. At the end of the day, DeFi's biggest strength lies in being able to cut out intermediaries and operate with zero censorship.

## Decentralized Finance vs. Traditional Finance

Friction, inaccessibility and regulatory uncertainties are some of the major issues plaguing the current banking system. It is unfortunate that not everyone is privileged to be banked in the current financial system - it is tough for the unbanked to compete on a level field.

The DeFi movement is about bridging these gaps, and making finance accessible to everyone without any form of censorship. In short, DeFi opens up huge windows of opportunities and allows users to access various financial instruments without any restriction on race, religion, age, nationality or geography.

When comparing both traditional and decentralized financial products, there will be pros and cons on each side. In this book, we will walk you through the concepts and possibilities of decentralized finance so you know how to use its best features to solve real-world problems.

In Chapter 2 we will provide an overview of DeFi along with some of its Decentralized Applications to help capture the underlying notions on how DeFi works.

## Recommended Readings

1. Decentralized Finance vs Traditional Finance: What You Need To Know (Stably) https://medium.com/stably-blog/decentralized-finance-vs-traditional-finance-what-you-need-to-know-3b57aed7a0c2
2. The 7 Major Flaws of the Global Financial System (Jeff Desjardins) https://www.visualcapitalist.com/7-major-flaws-global-financial-system
3. Decentralized Finance: An Emerging Alternative to the Global Financial System (Frank Cardona) https://www.visualcapitalist.com/decentralized-finance/
4. How Decentralized Finance Could Make Investing More Accessible (Jeff Desjardins) https://www.visualcapitalist.com/how-decentralized-finance-could-make-investing-more-accessible/

# CHAPTER 2: WHAT IS DECENTRALIZED FINANCE (DEFI)?

Decentralized Finance or DeFi is the movement that allows users to utilize financial services such as borrowing, lending, and trading without the need to rely on centralized entities. These financial services are provided via Decentralized Applications (Dapps), in which a majority of them are deployed on the Ethereum platform.

*While it is helpful to understand how Ethereum works to better visualize the ecosystem, you do not need to be an Ethereum expert to utilize the tools offered by DeFi. We will touch more on Ethereum in the next chapter.*

DeFi is not a single product or company but is instead a set of products and services that acts as a replacement for institutions ranging from banking, insurance, bonds and money markets. DeFi Dapps enable users to combine their services to open up multiple possibilities. It is often called money LEGOs due to its composability.

In order for DeFi Dapps to work, it usually requires collateral to be locked into smart contracts. The cumulative collateral locked in DeFi Dapps is often referred to as the Total Value Locked. According to DeFi Pulse, the Total Value Locked at the start of 2019 measured around $275 million but in February 2020, it reached a high of $1.2 billion. The large growth of Total Value Locked serves as an indicator of the rapid growth of the DeFi ecosystem.

## The DeFi Ecosystem

With such rapid growth, it would be impossible for us to cover everything DeFi has to offer in this book. That is why we have selected a few categories and DeFi Dapps that we believe are important and crucial for beginners to understand before stepping into the DeFi ecosystem.

These DeFi Dapps stand to revolutionize traditional financial services by removing the need for any middlemen. However, it should be noted that DeFi in its current state is still highly nascent and experimental with many projects being rapidly improved upon daily. As time goes on, DeFi may develop further and look entirely unrecognizable from what it is today. Nevertheless, it is useful to understand the early beginnings of DeFi and one can still take advantage of the features offered DeFi Dapps today with the right know-how.

## How Decentralized is DeFi?

It is not easy to answer how decentralized DeFi is. For simplicity's sake, we will separate the degrees of decentralization into three categories: centralized, semi-decentralized and completely decentralized.

1. Centralized
   o Characteristics: Custodial, uses centralized price feeds, centrally-determined interest rates, centrally-provided liquidity for margin calls
   o Examples: Salt, BlockFi, Nexo and Celsius
2. Semi-Decentralized (has one or more of these characteristics but not all)
   o Characteristics: Non-custodial, decentralized price feeds, permissionless initiation of margin calls, permissionless margin liquidity, decentralized interest rate determination, decentralized platform development/updates
   o Examples: Compound, MakerDAO, dYdX, bZx
3. Completely Decentralized
   o Characteristics: Every component is decentralized
   o Examples: No DeFi protocol is completely decentralized yet.

Currently, most DeFi dapps are sitting in the semi-decentralized category. A further breakdown of the decentralization components can be read in Kyle Kistner's article (https://hackernoon.com/how-decentralized-is-defi-a-framework-for-classifying-lending-protocols-90981f2c007f) in the Recommended Readings. Now that you have a better understanding of what being decentralized means, let's move on to key categories of DeFi.

## DeFi Key Categories

In this book, we will be covering the following 8 major categories of DeFi:

1. **Stablecoins**

   The prices of cryptocurrencies are known to be extremely volatile. It is common for cryptocurrencies to have intraday swings of over 10%. To mitigate this volatility, stablecoins that are pegged to other stable assets such as the USD were created.

   Tether (USDT) was one of the first centralized stablecoins to be introduced. Every USDT is supposedly backed by $1 in the issuer's bank account. However, one major downside to USDT is that users need to trust that the USD reserves are fully collateralized and actually exist.

   Decentralized stablecoins aim to solve this trust issue. Decentralized stablecoins are created in a decentralized manner via an overcollateralization method, operate fully on decentralized ledgers, are governed by decentralized autonomous organizations, and its reserves can be publicly audited by anyone.

   While stablecoins are not really a financial application themselves, they are important in making DeFi applications more accessible to everyone by having a stable store of value.

2. **Lending and Borrowing**

   Traditional financial systems require users to have bank accounts to utilize their services, a luxury that 1.7 billion people currently do not have. Borrowing from banks comes with other restrictions such as having a good credit score and having sufficient collateral to convince the banks that one is credit-worthy and able to repay a loan.

Decentralized lending and borrowing remove this barrier, allowing anyone to collateralize their digital assets and use this to obtain loans. One can also earn a yield on their assets and participate in the lending market by contributing to lending pools and earning interest on these assets. With decentralized lending and borrowing, there is no need for a bank account or a credit-worthiness check.

## 3. Exchanges

To exchange one cryptocurrency to another, one can use exchanges such as Coinbase or Binance. Exchanges like these are centralized exchanges, meaning they are both the intermediaries and custodians of the assets being traded. Users of these exchanges do not have full control of their assets, putting their assets at risk in case the exchanges get hacked and are unable to repay their obligations.

Decentralized exchanges aim to solve this issue by allowing users to exchange cryptocurrencies without giving up custody of their coins. Without storing any funds on centralized exchanges, users do not need to trust the exchanges to stay solvent.

## 4. Derivatives

A derivative is a contract whose value is derived from another underlying asset such as stocks, commodities, currencies, indexes, bonds, or interest rates.

Traders can use derivatives to hedge their positions and decrease their risk in any particular trade. For example, imagine you are a glove manufacturer and want to hedge yourself from an unexpected increase in rubber price. You can buy a futures contract from your supplier to deliver a specific amount of rubber at a specific future delivery date at an agreed price today.

Derivatives contracts are mainly traded on centralized platforms. DeFi platforms are starting to build decentralized derivatives markets. We will go through this in further detail in Chapter 8.

## 5. Fund Management

Fund management is the process of overseeing your assets and managing its cash flow to generate a return on your investments. There are two main types of fund management—active and passive fund management. Active fund management has a management team making investment decisions to beat a particular benchmark such as the S&P 500. Passive fund management does not have a management team but is designed in such a way to mimic the performance of a particular benchmark as closely as possible.

In DeFi, some projects have started to allow for passive fund management to take place in a decentralized manner. The transparency of DeFi makes it easy for users to track how their funds are being managed and understand the cost they will be paying.

## 6. Lottery

As DeFi continues to evolve, creative and disruptive financial applications will emerge, democratizing accessibility and removing intermediaries. Putting a DeFi spin onto lotteries allow for the removal of custodianship of the pooled capital unto a smart contract on the Ethereum Blockchain.

With the modularity of DeFi, it is possible to link a simple lottery Dapp to another DeFi Dapp and create something of more value. One DeFi Dapp that we will explore in this book allows participants to pool their capital together. The pooled capital is then invested into a DeFi lending Dapp and the interest earned is given to a random winner at a set interval. Once the winner is selected, the lottery purchasers get their lottery tickets refunded, ensuring no-loss to all participants.

7.  **Payments**

    A key role of cryptocurrency is to allow decentralized and trustless value transfer between two parties. With the growth of DeFi, more creative payment methods are being innovated and experimented.

    One such DeFi project that is explored in this book aims to change the way we approach payment by reconfiguring payments as streams instead of transactions we are familiar with. The possibility of providing payments as streams open up a plethora of potential applications of money. Imagine "pay-as-you-use" but on a much more granular scale and with higher accuracy.

    The nascency of DeFi and the rate of innovation will undoubtedly introduce new ways of thinking on how payments work to address many of the current financial system's shortfalls.

8.  **Insurance**

    Insurance is a risk management strategy in which an individual receives financial protection or reimbursement against losses from an insurance company in the event of an unfortunate incident. It is common for individuals to purchase insurance on cars, home, health, and life. But is there decentralized insurance for DeFi?

    All of the tokens locked within smart contracts are potentially vulnerable to smart contract exploits due to the large potential payout possible. While most projects have gotten their codebases audited, we never know if the smart contracts are truly safe and there is always a possibility of a hack which may result in a loss. The risks highlight the need for purchasing insurance especially if one is dealing with large amounts of funds on DeFi. We will explore several decentralized insurance options in this book.

## Recommended Readings

1. Decentralized Finance Explained (Yos Riady)
   https://yos.io/2019/12/08/decentralized-finance-explained/
2. A beginner's guide to DeFi (Linda J. Xie)
   https://nakamoto.com/beginners-guide-to-defi/
3. A Beginner's Guide to Decentralized Finance (DeFi) (Coinbase)
   https://blog.coinbase.com/a-beginners-guide-to-decentralized-finance-defi-574c68ff43c4
4. The Complete Beginner's Guide to Decentralized Finance (DeFi)
   (Binance) https://www.binance.vision/blockchain/the-complete-beginners-guide-to-decentralized-finance-defi
5. 2019 Was The Year of DeFi (and Why 2020 Will be Too) (Mason
   Nystrom) https://consensys.net/blog/news/2019-was-the-year-of-defi-and-why-2020-will-be-too/
6. DeFi: What It Is and Isn't (Part 1) (Justine Humenansky)
   https://medium.com/coinmonks/defi-what-it-is-and-isnt-part-1-f7d7e7afee16
7. How Decentralized is DeFi? A Framework for Classifying Lending
   Protocols (Kyle Kistner) https://hackernoon.com/how-decentralized-is-defi-a-framework-for-classifying-lending-protocols-90981f2c007f
8. How Decentralized is "Decentralized Finance"? (Aaron Hay)
   https://medium.com/coinmonks/how-decentralized-is-decentralized-finance-89aea3070e8f
9. Mapping Decentralized Finance https://outlierventures.io/wp-content/uploads/2019/06/Mapping-Decentralised-Finance-DeFi-report.pdf
10. Market Report: 2019 DeFi Year in Review
    https://defirate.com/market-report-2019/
11. DeFi #3 – 2020: The Borderless State of DeFi
    https://research.binance.com/analysis/2020-borderless-state-of-defi
12. Decentralized Finance with Tom Schmidt (Software Engineering
    Daily)
    https://softwareengineeringdaily.com/2020/02/25/decentralized-finance-with-tom-schmidt/

# PART TWO: GETTING INTO DEFI

# CHAPTER 3: THE DECENTRALIZED LAYER: ETHEREUM

## What is Ethereum?

As mentioned in Chapter 1, the majority of the DeFi Dapps are currently being built on the Ethereum blockchain. But what exactly is Ethereum? Ethereum is a global, open-source platform for decentralized applications. You can think of it as a world computer that cannot be shut down. On Ethereum, software developers can write smart contracts that control digital value through a set of criteria and are accessible anywhere in the world.

In this book specifically, we will be exploring Decentralized Applications (Dapps) that provide financial services known as DeFi. Smart contracts that are written by software programmers are the building blocks of these Dapps. These smart contracts are then deployed to the Ethereum network, where it will run 24/7. The network will maintain the digital value and keep track of the latest state.

## What is a Smart Contract?

A smart contract is a programmable contract that allows two counterparties to set conditions of a transaction without needing to trust another third party for the execution.

For example, if Alice wants to set up a trust fund to pay Bob $100 at the start of each month for the next 12 months, she can program a smart contract to:
1. Check the current date
2. At the start of each month, send Bob $100 automatically
3. Repeat until the fund in the smart contract is exhausted

Using a smart contract, Alice has bypassed the need to have a trusted third-party intermediary (lawyers, escrow agents etc) to send the trust fund to Bob and made the process transparent to all involved parties.

Smart contracts work on the "if this, then that" principle. Whenever a certain condition is fulfilled, the smart contract will carry out the operation as programmed.

Multiple smart contracts are combined to operate with each other, which would be known as decentralized application (Dapp) in order to fulfill more complex processes and computation.

## What is Ether (ETH)?
Ether is the native currency of the Ethereum blockchain.

It is like money and can be used for everyday transactions similar to Bitcoin. You can send Ether to another person to purchase goods and services based on the current market value. The Ethereum blockchain records the transfer and ensures the finality of the transaction.

Besides that, Ether is also used to pay for the fee that allows smart contracts and Dapps to run on the Ethereum network. You can think of executing smart contracts on the Ethereum network as driving a car. To drive a car, you require fuel. To execute a smart contract on Ethereum, you need to use Ether to pay a fee known as Gas.

Ether is slowly evolving to become its own unique reserve currency and store of value. Currently, within the DeFi ecosystem, Ether is the preferred asset choice used as the collateral underlying many DeFi Dapps. It provides safety and transparency to this financial system. If this confuses you, do not worry as we will be covering this topic in further depth throughout this book.

## What is Gas?

On Ethereum, all transactions and smart contract executions require a small fee to be paid. This fee is called Gas. In technical terms, Gas refers to the unit of measure on the amount of computational effort required to execute an operation or a smart contract. The more complex the execution operation is, the more gas is required to fulfill that operation. Gas fees are paid entirely in ETH.

The price of gas can fluctuate from time to time depending on the network demand. If there are more people interacting on the Ethereum blockchain such as transacting in ETH or executing smart contract operations, due to the limited amount of computing resources on the network, Gas price can increase. Conversely when the network is underutilized, the market price of gas would decrease.

Gas fees can be set manually, and in a situation where the network is congested due to high utilization, transactions with the highest gas fee associated with it will be prioritized for validation. Validated transactions will be finalized and added to the blockchain. If gas fees paid are too low, the transactions will be queued up which can take a while to complete. Therefore, transactions with lower-than-average gas fees can take much longer to complete.

---

Gas price is typically denoted in *gwei*.
1 *gwei* = 0.000000001 ether

Assume a smart contract execution to transfer tokens require 21,000 gas units.
Assume the average market rate for gas price is 3 *gwei*.

21,000 gas x 3 gwei = 63,000 gwei = 0.000063 ETH

---

When executing the transactions, you will pay a gas fee of 0.000063 ETH to process and validate your transaction in the network.

*Example of how gas fees are calculated*

## What are Decentralized Applications (Dapps)?

In the context of Ethereum, Dapps are interfaces that interact with the blockchain through the use of smart contracts. From the front, Dapps look and behave like regular web and mobile applications, except that they interact with a blockchain and in different ways. Some of the ways include requiring ETH to use the Dapp, storage of user data onto blockchain such that it is immutable, and so on.

## What are the benefits of Dapps?

Dapps are built on top of decentralized blockchain networks such as Ethereum and usually have the following benefits:

- **Immutability:** Nobody can change any information once it's on the blockchain.
- **Tamper-proof:** Smart contracts published onto the blockchain cannot be tampered with without alerting every other participant on the blockchain.
- **Transparent:** Smart contracts powering Dapps are openly auditable.
- **Availability:** As long as the Ethereum network remains active, Dapps built on it will remain active and usable.

## What are the disadvantages of Dapps?

While a blockchain offers many benefits, there are also many different downsides that come along with it:

- **Immutability:** Smart contracts are written by humans and can only be as good as the person who wrote it. Human errors are unavoidable and immutable smart contracts have the potential to compound errors into something larger.
- **Transparent:** Openly auditable smart contracts can also become attack vectors for hackers as they can view the code to find exploits.

26

- **Scalability:** In most cases, the bandwidth of a Dapp is limited to the blockchain it resides on.

## What else can Ethereum be used for?

Besides creating Dapps, Ethereum can be used for two other functions: creating Decentralized Autonomous Organizations (DAO) or issuing other cryptocurrencies.

A DAO is a fully autonomous organization which is not governed by a single person but is instead governed through code. This code is based on smart contracts and enables DAOs to replace how traditional organizations are typically run. As it runs on code, it would be protected from human intervention and will operate transparently. There would be no effect by any outside influence. Governance decisions or rulings would be decided via DAO token voting.

Speaking of tokens, Ethereum can be used as a platform to create other cryptocurrencies. There are currently two popular protocols for tokens on the Ethereum Network: ERC-20 and ERC-721. ERC-20 is a protocol standard that defines rules and standards for issuing tokens on Ethereum. ERC-20 tokens are fungible, meaning they are interchangeable and of the same value. On the other hand, ERC-721 tokens are non-fungible, meaning it is completely unique and non-interchangeable. A simple analogy would be to think of ERC-20 as money and ERC-721 as collectibles like action figures or baseball cards.

And that's it for Ethereum—if you're keen to own your first cryptocurrency or try your first Dapp, we will be covering several interesting DeFi products which include overviews and step-by-step guides. But before you begin your journey, you will need an Ethereum Wallet!

**Recommended Readings**

1. What is Ethereum? [The Most Updated Step-by-Step-Guide!] (Ameer Rosic) https://blockgeeks.com/guides/ethereum/
2. Smart Contracts: The Blockchain Technology That Will Replace Lawyers (Ameer Rosic) https://blockgeeks.com/guides/smart-contracts/
3. What is Ethereum Gas? [The Most Comprehensive Step-By-Step Guide Ever!] (Ameer Rosic) https://blockgeeks.com/guides/ethereum-gas/
4. The trillion-dollar case for ETH (Lucas Campbell) https://bankless.substack.com/p/the-trillion-dollar-case-for-eth-eb6
5. Ethereum: The Digital Finance Stack (David Hoffman) https://medium.com/pov-crypto/ethereum-the-digital-finance-stack-4ba988c6c14b
6. Ether: A New Model for Money (David Hoffman) https://medium.com/pov-crypto/ether-a-new-model-for-money-17365b5535ba

# CHAPTER 4: ETHEREUM WALLETS

A wallet is a user-friendly interface to the blockchain network. It manages your private keys, which are basically keys to the lock on your cryptocurrencies' vault. Wallets allow you to receive, store and send cryptocurrencies.

## Custodial vs Non-Custodial

There are two kinds of wallets, custodial and non-custodial wallets. Custodial wallets are wallets where third-parties keep and maintain control over your cryptocurrencies on your behalf. Non-custodial wallets are wallets where you take full control and ownership of your cryptocurrencies. This is similar to the mantra espoused by many people in the blockchain industry to "be your own bank".

By using a custodial wallet, you trust an external party to store your coins safely. This may be convenient as you do not need to worry about private key security but you only have to worry about account credentials security just like how you would have to protect your email account. However, by trusting a third party with your cryptocurrencies, you open yourself up to the risk of the custodian losing your cryptocurrencies through mismanagement or hacks. There have been numerous incidents of custodial wallets losing their cryptocurrencies with the most prominent example being Mt. Gox lost over 850,000 bitcoin worth over $450 million in 2014.

By using a non-custodial wallet, you trust no external party and only yourself to ensure that your cryptocurrencies are safe. However, by using a non-custodial wallet, you pass the burden of security to yourself and you have to be fully equipped to store your private keys safely. If you lose your private keys, you will lose access to your cryptocurrencies too.

At CoinGecko, we believe in the "not your keys, not your coin" mantra. We believe that you should educate yourself in all the best security practices and trust only yourself to keep your coins safe.

## Which Wallet Should I Use?

There are many cryptocurrency wallets out there in the market. For the purposes of this book, we will walk you through two DeFi friendly wallets for you to easily start interacting with the Ethereum network.

## Mobile Users: Argent

For mobile users, you may consider using Argent wallet. Argent is a non-custodial wallet that offers ease-of-use and high security, something that does not always go hand-in-hand. It does so by utilizing Argent Guardians, which are people, devices, or third-party services that can verify your identity.

Examples include family and friends who are also Argent users, other hardware or Metamask wallets, or two-factor authentication services. By utilizing this limited circle of trust network, Argent is rethinking the need for paper-based seed phrase backups when recovering accounts.

Argent Guardians allows you to lock your wallet and instantly freeze all funds in the event you believe your wallet has been compromised. Your wallet will be automatically unlocked after 5 days or you can request for your Argent Guardian to unlock it sooner.

You may also set additional security measures to improve your wallet security such as a daily transaction limit. This is useful in preventing hackers from siphoning funds from your Argent wallet in the case they gain access to your wallet. Whenever your daily transaction limit is hit, you will receive a notification and any transactions over the limit are delayed for over 24 hours. You can of course authorize legitimate large transactions over the limit through the help of your Argent Guardians.

Argent offers free transactions for wallet users and absorbs all Ethereum gas fees that need to be paid to the network. With Argent wallet, you can easily interact with DeFi Dapps directly from the wallet without the need to use another app or device.

## Pro Tip

*There is currently a waiting list to use Argent Wallet. To skip the queue, you may use this link (non-sponsored) to sign up:* <u>*https://argent.link/coingecko*</u>

## Argent: Step-by-Step Guide

Step 1
- Go to <u>https://argent.link/coingecko</u>
- Download the app on your mobile phone

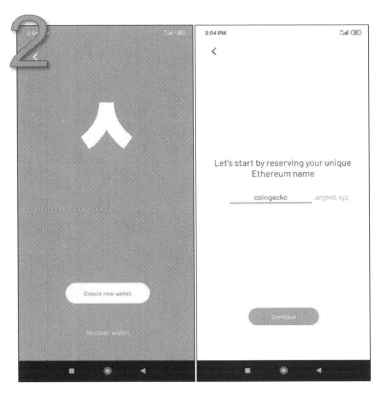

Step 2

- Once downloaded, choose a unique Ethereum name for your argent wallet

Step 3
- Argent will ask if you want to add your phone number for added security and verification purposes

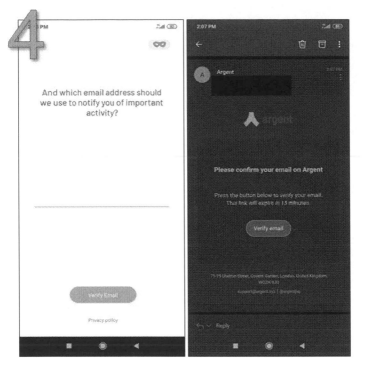

Step 4
- Afterward, Argent will ask for your email for verification purposes.

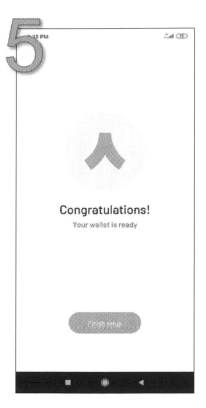

Step 5
- You will be on the waitlist. To skip the queue, you may use this link to sign up: https://argent.link/coingecko
- You will get an email notification once your wallet is ready to use!

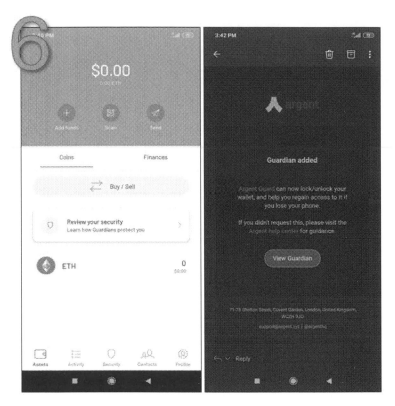

Step 6

- You start depositing or sending cryptocurrencies to other people. Do consider adding additional Argent Guardians to improve your security.

## Desktop Users: Metamask

For desktop users, you may use Metamask, a web browser extension available on the Chrome, Firefox, Opera, and Brave browsers. Like Argent, Metamask is a non-custodial wallet and it acts as both a wallet and an interaction bridge for the Ethereum network.

You can store your Ethereum and ERC20 tokens on Metamask. Acting as an interaction bridge, Metamask enables you to use all Decentralized Applications (Dapps) that are hosted on the Ethereum Network.

Without the use of an interaction bridge like MetaMask, your browser would not be able to access the Ethereum blockchain unless you were running a full Ethereum node and have the entire Ethereum blockchain of over 400GB downloaded on your computer. On a technical level, MetaMask does this by injecting a javascript library known as web3.js written by the core Ethereum developers into your browser's page to enable you to easily interact with the Ethereum network.

Metamask makes interaction with DeFi Dapps on the Ethereum network very convenient on your laptop or PC. They are secured to some degree as it requires you to sign each interaction and transaction you execute on the network.

However, you must take precautions to keep your Metamask safe and secure. Anybody who has your password or seed phrase (a secret phrase given to you during wallet sign-up) will have complete control of your wallet.

Most DeFi Dapps can be accessed using Metamask and in the later chapters, you will notice that the step-by-step guides have been completed using Metamask.

**Metamask: Step-by-Step Guide**

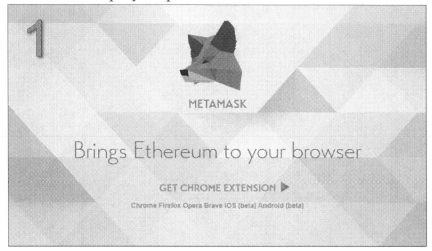

Step 1

- Go to https://metamask.io/
- Download extension for the browser of your choice

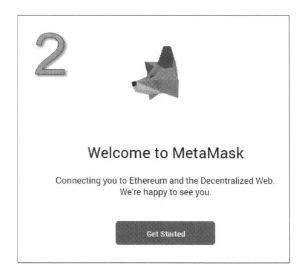

Step 2

- After you have downloaded the extension, click "Get Started"

## Step 3

- Click "Create a Wallet" and click "Next".

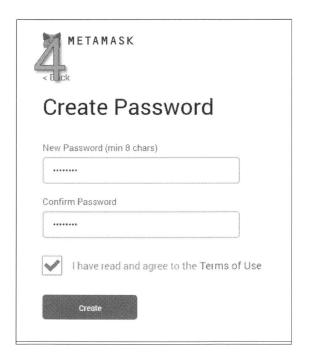

## Step 4

- Create your password.

**5** METAMASK

# Secret Backup Phrase

Your secret backup phrase makes it easy to back up and restore your account.

WARNING: Never disclose your backup phrase. Anyone with this phrase can take your Ether forever.

CLICK HERE TO REVEAL SECRET WORDS

Tips:

Store this phrase in a password manager like 1Password.

Write this phrase on a piece of paper and store in a secure location. If you want even more security, write it down on multiple pieces of paper and store each in 2 - 3 different locations.

Memorize this phrase.

Download this Secret Backup Phrase and keep it stored safely on an external encrypted hard drive or storage medium.

Remind me later

NEXT

Step 5 (IMPORTANT! READ CAREFULLY!)

- You will be given a Secret Backup Phrase
- NEVER lose it
- NEVER show it to anyone
- If you lose the phrase, you can't retrieve it
- If anyone else has it, they are able to access your wallet and do anything with it

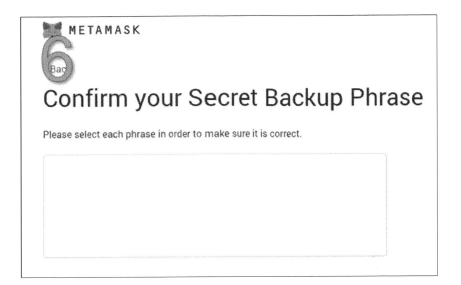

Step 6

- You will be prompted to write the given secret backup phrase to confirm that you have noted it down

# Congratulations

You passed the test - keep your seedphrase safe, it's your responsibility!

**Tips on storing it safely**

- Save a backup in multiple places.
- Never share the phrase with anyone.
- Be careful of phishing! MetaMask will never spontaneously ask for your seed phrase.
- If you need to back up your seed phrase again, you can find it in Settings -> Security.
- If you ever have questions or see something fishy, email support@metamask.io.

*MetaMask cannot recover your seedphrase. Learn more.

Step 7

- Congratulations! Your wallet is now created! You can use it to store Ethereum and ERC20 tokens

Step 8

- Below is your public key or your Ethereum address to your wallet
- Your QR code can be scanned if anyone wants to send you coins.

## Recommended Readings

1. Argent: The quick start guide (Matthew Wright) https://medium.com/argenthqargent-the-quick-start-guide-13541ce2b1fb
2. A new era for crypto security (Itamar Lesuisse) https://medium.com/argenthq/a-new-era-for-crypto-security-57909a095ae3
3. A Complete Beginner's Guide to Using MetaMask (Ian Lee) https://www.coingecko.com/buzz/complete-beginners-guide-to-metamask
4. MyCrypto's Security Guide For Dummies And Smart People Too (Taylor Monahan) https://medium.com/mycrypto/mycryptos-security-guide-for-dummies-and-smart-people-too-ab178299c82e

# PART THREE: DEEP DIVING INTO DEFI

# CHAPTER 5: DECENTRALIZED STABLECOINS

The prices of cryptocurrencies are extremely volatile. To mitigate this volatility, stablecoins that are pegged to other stable assets such as the USD were created. Stablecoins help users to hedge against this price volatility and was created to be a reliable medium of exchange. Stablecoins have since quickly evolved to be a strong component of DeFi that is pivotal to this modular ecosystem.

There are 19 stablecoins currently listed on CoinGecko. The top 5 stablecoins has a market capitalization totaling over $5 billion.

| Top 5 Cryptocurrency Stablecoins (Feb 2020) | | |
|------|------|------|
| Rank | Bank | Market Cap. ($ million) |
| 1 | Tether (USDT) | 4,284 |
| 2 | USD Coin (USDC) | 443 |
| 3 | Paxos Standard (PAX) | 202 |
| 4 | True USD (TUSD) | 142 |
| 5 | Dai (DAI) | 123 |

*Source: CoinGecko.com*

We will be looking into USD-pegged stablecoins in this chapter. Not all stablecoins are the same as they employ different mechanisms to keep their peg against USD. There are two types of pegs, namely fiat-collateralized and crypto-collateralized. Most stablecoins employ the fiat-collateralized system to maintain their USD peg.

For simplicity, we will look at two USD stablecoins, Tether (USDT) and Dai (DAI) to showcase the differences in their pegging management.

Tether (USDT) pegs itself to $1 by maintaining reserves of $1 per Tether token minted. While Tether is the largest and most widely used USD stablecoin with daily trading volumes averaging approximately $30 billion in the month of January 2020, Tether reserves are kept in financial institutions and users will have to trust Tether as an entity to actually have the reserve amounts that they claim. Tether is therefore a **centralized, fiat-collateralized stablecoin**.

Dai (DAI) on the other hand, is collateralized using cryptocurrencies such as Ethereum (ETH). Its value is pegged to $1 through protocols voted on by a decentralized autonomous organization and smart contracts. At any given time, the collateral to generate DAI can be easily validated by users. DAI is a **decentralized, crypto-collateralized stablecoin**.

Based on the top 5 stablecoins' market capitalization, Tether dominates the stablecoin market with approximately 80% of market share. Although DAI's market share only stands at about 3%, its trading volume has been increasing at a much faster rate. DAI's trading volume increased by over 4,000% relative to Tether's growth of 126% since the start of January 2020.

DAI is the native stablecoin used most widely in the DeFi ecosystem. It is the preferred USD stablecoin used in DeFi trading, lending and more. To understand DAI further, we will introduce you to its platform, Maker.

## Maker

### What is Maker?

Maker is a smart-contract platform that runs on the Ethereum blockchain and **has three tokens**: stablecoins, Sai and Dai (both algorithmically pegged to $1), as well as its governance token, Maker (MKR).

**Sai (SAI)** is also known as Single Collateral Dai and is backed only by Ether (ETH) as collateral.

**Dai (DAI)** was launched in November 2019 and is also known as Multi-Collateral Dai. It is currently backed by Ether (ETH) and Basic Attention Token (BAT) as collaterals with plans to add other assets as collaterals in the future.

**Maker (MKR)** is Maker's governance token and users can use it to vote for improvements on the Maker platform via the Maker Improvement Proposals. Maker is a type of organization known as a Decentralized Autonomous Organization (DAO). We will look further into this under the governance subsection.

### What are the Differences between Sai and Dai?

Maker initially started out on 19 December 2017 with the Single Collateral Dai. It was minted using Ether (ETH) as the sole collateral. On 18 November 2019, Maker announced the launch of the new Multi-Collateral Dai, which can be minted using either Ether (ETH) and/or Basic Attention Token (BAT) as collateral, with plans to allow other cryptocurrencies to back it in the future. To reiterate,

| | | | | |
|---|---|---|---|---|
| Single-Collateral Dai | = | Legacy Dai | = | Sai |
| Multi-Collateral Dai | = | New Dai | = | Dai |

Moving forward, Multi-Collateral Dai will be the de-facto stablecoin standard maintained by Maker and eventually, SAI will be phased out and no longer supported by Maker. For brevity, we will only be using Multi-Collateral Dai (DAI) to walk through examples in the following sections.

## How does Maker Govern the System?

Recall our brief mention on Decentralized Autonomous Organization (DAO)? That's where the Maker (MKR) token comes in. MKR holders have voting rights proportional to the amount of MKR tokens they own in the DAO and can vote on parameters governing the Maker Protocol.

The parameters that the MKR holders vote on are vital in keeping the ecosystem healthy, which in turn helps ensure that Dai remains pegged to $1. We will briefly go through three key parameters which you will need to know in the Dai stablecoin ecosystem:

I.   Collateral Ratio

The amount of Dai that can be minted is dependent on the collateral ratio.

| | | |
|---|---|---|
| Ether (ETH) collateral ratio | = | 150% |
| Basic Attention Token (BAT) collateral ratio | = | 150% |

Essentially, what it means with a collateral ratio of 150% is that to mint $100, you need to deposit a minimum of $150 worth of ETH or BAT.

II.  Stability Fee

It is equivalent to the 'interest rate' which you are required to pay along with the principal debt of the vault. The stability fee is at 8% as of February 2020.

III. Dai Savings Rate (DSR)

The Dai Savings Rate (DSR) is the interest earned by holding Dai over time. It also acts as a monetary tool to influence the demand of Dai. The DSR rate is set at 7.50% as of February 2020.

**Motivations to Issue DAI:**

Why would you *want* to lock up a higher value of ETH or BAT only to issue Dai with a lower value? You could have sold your assets directly to USD instead.

There are three possible cases:

I.  You need cash now and you have an asset that you believe will be worth more in the future.
    - In this case, you could hold your asset in the Maker vault and get the money now by issuing Dai.

II. You need cash now but do not want to risk triggering a taxable event when selling your asset.
    - Instead, you will draw the loans by issuing Dai.

III. Investment Leverage
    - You are able to conduct investment leverage on your assets given that you believe the value of your assets would go up.

## How do I get my hands on some Dai (DAI)?

There are two ways you can get your hands on some Dai (DAI):

1. Minting Dai

   We will walk through how DAI can be minted using a pawnshop analogy.

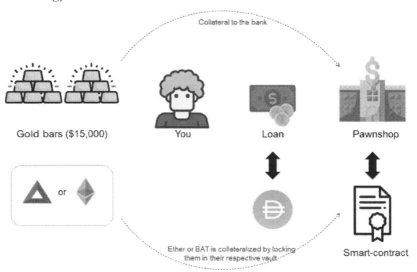

Let's assume that one day you are in need of $10,000 cash, but all you have are gold bars worth $15,000 at home. Believing that the price of gold will increase in the future, instead of selling the gold bars for cash, you decide to go to a pawnshop to borrow $10,000 cash by putting your gold bars as collateral for it. The pawnshop agrees to lend you $10,000 with an interest of 8% for the cash loan. Both of you sign a contract agreement to finalize the transaction.

Now let's change the terminology to get the narrative of DAI:

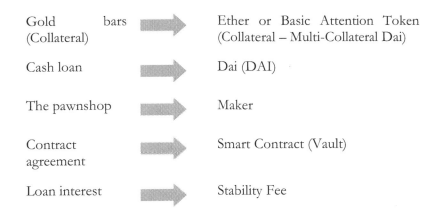

| | |
|---|---|
| Gold bars (Collateral) | Ether or Basic Attention Token (Collateral – Multi-Collateral Dai) |
| Cash loan | Dai (DAI) |
| The pawnshop | Maker |
| Contract agreement | Smart Contract (Vault) |
| Loan interest | Stability Fee |

What happens is that you will mint or 'borrow' Dai via the Maker platform by putting your Ether (ETH) or Basic Attention Token (BAT) as collateral. You will have to repay your 'loan' along with the 'loan interest' which is the stability fee when you want to redeem your ETH or BAT at the end of your loan.

To provide an overview, let's walk through how you can mint your own Dai.

On the Maker platform (www.oasis.app), you can borrow Dai by putting your ETH or BAT into the vault. Assuming ETH is currently worth $150, you can thus lock 1 ETH into the vault and receive a maximum of 100 DAI ($100) with a 150% collateral ratio.

You should not draw out the maximum of 100 DAI that you are allowed to but leave some buffer in the event that ETH price decreases. It is advisable to give a wider gap to ensure your collateral ratio always remains above 150%. This ensures that your vault will not be liquidated and charged the 13% liquidation penalty in the event that ETH falls in price and your collateral ratio falls below 150%.

## 2. Trading DAI

The above methods are all the ways DAI are created. Once DAI is created, you can send it anywhere you want. Some users may send their DAI to cryptocurrency exchanges and you may also buy DAI from these secondary markets without the need to mint them.

Buying DAI this way is easier as you don't have to lock up collateral and do not have to worry about the collateral ratio and stability fee.

We will keep this section brief—you can check out CoinGecko for the list of exchanges that trades DAI.

## Black Swan Event

A black swan event is an unpredictable and extreme event that may cause severe consequences. In the case where both ETH and BAT has a significant drop in price, Emergency Shutdown is triggered. It is a process used as a last resort to settle the Maker Platform by shutting the system down. The process is to ensure the holders of Dai holders and Vault users receive the net value of assets they are entitled to.

## Why use Maker?

As previously mentioned in Section 2: Stablecoins, there are many stablecoins out there and the core distinctions of these coins lie in their protocol. Unlike most stablecoin platforms, Maker is **fully** operating on the distributed ledger. Thus, Maker inherently possesses the characteristics of the blockchain: secured, immutable and most importantly, transparent. Additionally, Maker's infrastructures have strengthened the security of the system with comprehensive risk protocols and mechanisms via real-time information.

And that's it for Makers' Stablecoin, Dai—if you're keen to get started or test it out, we've included step-by-step guides on how to (i) mint some DAI for yourself and (ii) save DAI to earn interest. Otherwise, head on to the next section to read more on the next DeFi app!

## Maker: Step-by-Step Guides
Minting your own DAI

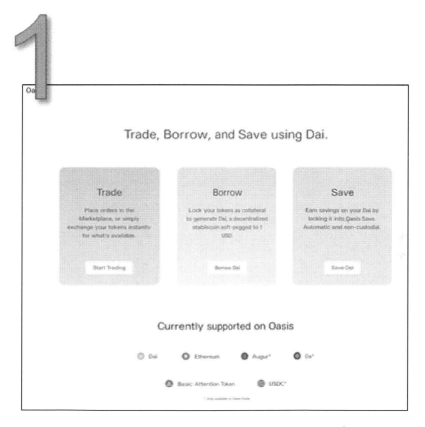

Step 1
- Go to https://oasis.app/
- Click Borrow
- You will be asked to connect your wallet. Connecting your wallet is free, all you need to do is sign a transaction

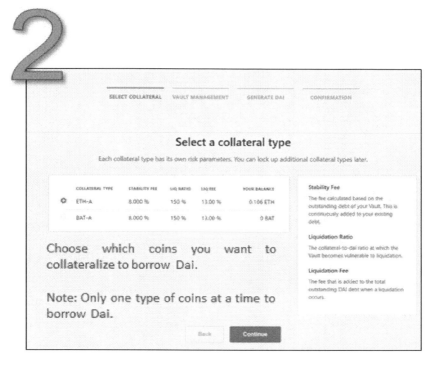

Step 2
- Click "Start Borrow" once you are on the borrow page (https://oasis.app/borrow/)
- Choose which cryptoasset you want to lock-in (collateralize)

Step 3

- In this example, I chose to lock-in ETH
- Insert any amount you wish to lock. Note: You have to lock an equal amount of 20 DAI and above. (ie: You can't borrow DAI less than 20 DAI)
- Click Continue and follow the instructions afterward

Step 4
- Congratulations! Your ETH vault is now created!

In addition to minting DAI, you can also save on Maker's platform to earn interest on your assets. We've prepared a step-by-step guide on how to save your DAI below:

## Saving your DAI

### Step 1

- Navigate to the Save page on the left sidebar (https://oasis.app/save)

### Step 2

- Click Start Save
- Enter the amount of DAI you wish to save
- Click deposit
- Confirm in wallet

Step 3
- And it's done!
- Note: You only have one DSR account. If you were to deposit more DAI after your first deposit, it will be added to it.

## Recommended Readings

1. Maker Protocol 101 (Maker) https://docs.makerdao.com/maker-protocol-101
2. Maker for Dummies: A Plain English Explanation of the Dai Stablecoin (Gregory DiPrisco) https://medium.com/cryptolinks/maker-for-dummies-a-plain-english-explanation-of-the-dai-stablecoin-e4481d79b90
3. What's MakerDAO and what's going on with it? Explained with pictures. (Kerman Kohli) https://hackernoon.com/whats-makerdao-and-what-s-going-on-with-it-explained-with-pictures-f7ebf774e9c2
4. How to get a DAI saving account (Ryan Sean Adams) https://bankless.substack.com/p/how-to-get-a-dai-saving-account

# CHAPTER 6: DECENTRALIZED LENDING AND BORROWING

One of the most common services offered by the financial industry is the lending and borrowing of funds, which was made possible by the concept of credit and collateralization.

It can be argued that the invention of commercial-scale lending and borrowing was what brought about the Renaissance age as the possibility for the less wealthy to acquire startup funds led to a flurry of economic activity. Thus, the economy began to grow at an unprecedented pace.[9]

Entrepreneurs can borrow the upfront capital needed to establish a business by collateralizing the business while families can get a mortgage for a house that would otherwise be too costly to buy in cash, whilst using the house as collateral. On the other hand, the wealth accumulated can be lent off as capital to lenders. This system reduces the risk of borrowers absconding with the borrowed funds.

However, this system requires some form of trust and an intermediary. The role of an intermediary is taken up by banks and trust is maintained via a convoluted system of credit, whereby the borrower must exhibit the ability to repay the loan in order to be qualified to borrow, among a laundry list of other qualifications and requirements by the banks.

---

[9] "Sapiens - Google Books." 4 Sep. 2014,
https://books.google.com/books/about/Sapiens.html?id=1EiJAwAAQBAJ.

This has led to various challenges and shortfalls of the current lending and borrowing system, such as restrictive funding criteria, geographical or legal restriction to access banks, high barriers to loan acceptance, and the exclusivity of only the wealthy to enjoy the benefits of low-risk high-returns lending.

In the DeFi landscape, such barriers do not exist as banks are no longer necessary. With enough collateral, anyone can have access to capital to do whatever they want. Capital lending is also something that is no longer enjoyed only by the wealthy, everyone can contribute to a decentralized liquidity pool of which borrowers can take from and pay back at an algorithmically-determined interest rate. In contrast to applying for a loan from the bank where there are stringent Know-your-customer (KYC) and Anti-money laundering (AML) policies, one only needs to provide collateral to take a loan in DeFi.

We will explore just how such bankless lending and borrowing mechanism is possible with Compound Finance, a Defi lending and borrowing protocol.

## Compound

Compound Finance is an Ethereum-based open-source money market protocol where anyone can **supply or borrow cryptocurrencies** frictionlessly. As of Feb 2020, 7 different tokens—Basic Attention Token (BAT), Dai (DAI), (Ether (ETH), Augur (REP), USD Coin (USDC), Wrapped Bitcoin (WBTC) and 0x (ZRX)—can be supplied or used as collateral on the Compound Platform.

Compound operates as a liquidity pool that is built on the Ethereum blockchain. Suppliers supply assets to the pool and earn interest, while borrowers take a loan from the pool and pay interest on their debt. In essence, Compound bridges the gaps between lenders who wish to accrue interest from idle funds and borrowers who wish to borrow funds for productive or investment use.

In Compound, interest rates are denoted in Annual Percentage Yield (APY) and differ between assets. Compound derives the interest rates for different assets through algorithms which account for supply and demand of the asset.

Essentially, Compound lowers the friction for lending/borrowing by allowing suppliers/borrowers to interact directly with the protocol for interest rates without needing to negotiate loan terms (eg. maturity, interest rate, counterparty, collaterals), thereby creating a more efficient money market.

### How much interest will you receive, or pay?

The Annual Percentage Yield (APY) differs between assets as it is algorithmically set based on the supply and demand of the asset. Generally, the higher the borrowing demand, the higher the interest rate (APY) and vice versa.

| All Markets | | | | |
|---|---|---|---|---|
| Market | Gross Supply | Supply APY | Gross Borrow | Borrow APY |
| Ether ETH | $98.42M +3.02% | 0.01% -- | $770k +1.17% | 2.10% -- |
| Dai DAI | $32.57M -0.95% | 7.58% -- | $17.50M +1.39% | 8.00% -- |
| USD Coin USDC | $26.86M -0.80% | 5.48% +0.36 | $17.65M +3.00% | 8.92% +0.26 |

Using the DAI stablecoin as an example, a lender would earn 7.58% (as of Feb 2020) in a year while a borrower would be paying 8.00% interest after a year.

**Do I need to register for an account to start using Compound?**
No, you do not need to register for an account and that's the beauty of Decentralized Finance applications! Unlike traditional financial applications where users are required to go through lengthy processes to get started, Compound users do not need to register for anything.

Anyone with a supported cryptocurrency wallet such as Argent and Metamask can start using Compound immediately.

**Start earning interest on Compound**
To earn interest, you will have to supply assets to the protocol. As of February 2020, Compound accepts 7 types of tokens.

Once you have deposited your asset into Compound, you will immediately begin to earn interest on the assets you have put in! Interest accrued on the amount that you have supplied and is calculated after each Ethereum block (average ~13 seconds).

Upon deposit, you will receive corresponding amounts of cTokens. If you supply DAI, you will receive cDAI, if you supply Ether, you will receive cETH, and so on). Interest is not immediately distributed to you, but rather accrues on the cTokens which you now hold and are redeemable for the underlying asset and interest it represents.

**cTokens?**
cTokens represent your balance in the protocol and accrue interest over time. In Compound, interest earned is not distributed immediately but is instead accrued in cTokens.

Let's go through this with an **example.** Assume that you have supplied 1,000 DAI on 1 January 2019 and APY has been constant at 10.00% throughout 2019.

On 1 January 2019, after you have deposited 1,000 DAI, you will be given 1,000 cDAI. In this case, the exchange rate between DAI and cDAI is 1:1.

On 1 January 2020, after 1 year, your 1,000 cDAI will now increase in value by 10%. The new exchange rate between DAI and cDAI is 1:1.1. Your 1,000 cDAI is now redeemable for 1,100 DAI.

---

**1 Jan 2019:** Deposit 1,000 DAI. Receive 1,000 cDAI. Exchange Rate: 1 cDAI = 1 DAI

**1 Jan 2020:** Redeem 1,000 cDAI. Receive 1,100 DAI. Exchange Rate: 1 cDAI = 1.1 DAI (cDAI value increased by 10%)

---

To account for the interest accrued, cTokens become convertible into an increasing amount of the underlying asset it represents over time. cTokens are also ERC-20 tokens, meaning you can easily transfer the "ownership" of supplied assets if someone wants to take over your position as a supplier.

## Start borrowing on Compound

Before borrowing, you have to supply assets into the system as collateral for your loan. Each asset has a different collateral factor. The more assets you supply, the greater is your borrowing power.

Borrowed assets are sent directly to your Ethereum wallet and from there, you can use them as you would any cryptoasset—anything you want to! Do note that that borrowing incurs a small fee of 0.025% to avoid spams and misuse of the Compound protocol.

## Price movement of collateral asset

If you're thinking about putting in collateral to take a loan, you may be wondering—what happens if the value of the collateral changes? Let's see:

1.  Collateral value moves up
    If the value of the asset you used as collateral goes up, your collateral ratio also goes up, which is fine - nothing will happen and you can draw a bigger loan if you'd like to.

2.  Collateral value moves down

    On the other hand, if the collateral goes down such that your collateral ratio is now below the required collateral ratio, your collateral will be partially sold off along with a 5% liquidation fee. The process of selling off your collateral so that you achieve the minimum collateral ratio is known as liquidation.

## Liquidation

Liquidation occurs when the value of the collateral provided is less than the borrowed funds. This is to ensure that there is always excess liquidity for withdrawal and borrowing of funds, meanwhile protect lenders against default risk. The current liquidation fee is 5%.

And that's it for Compound - if you're keen to get started or test it out, we've included step-by-step guides on how to (i) supply funds to the pool and (ii) borrow from the pool. Otherwise, head on to the next section to read more on the next DeFi app!

## Compound.Finance: Step-by-Step Guides

Supplying fund to the pool:

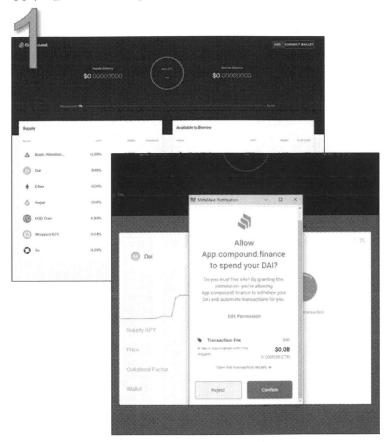

Step 1
- Head over to https://app.compound.finance
- Connect your wallet. Follow your wallet's instructions
- Deposit cryptocurrencies into the liquidity pool (any of the 7 tokens)

Step 2

- Receive cTokens
- When you sign up for a fixed deposit, the bank will issue a fixed deposit certificate as proof of placement. Similarly, after supplying assets, you will get cTokens which represent the type and amount of assets you have deposited
- The cTokens act as a claim of deposit and record the interest you earn. Likewise, you have to use it to redeem or withdraw your assets

## Step 3

- Earn Interest
- The moment you deposit assets, you start to earn interest. By holding the cTokens, the interest will accrue on your account.

## Step 4

- Redeem cToken
- Over time, the interest accumulates and each cTokens is convertible into a greater value of underlying assets. You can redeem the cTokens anytime and receive the assets back to your wallet instantly.

Borrowing fund from the pool:

Note:

- Before you could start borrowing, you are required to supply a value worth of assets into the compound as a form of collateral.
- Each token has its own collateral factor. A collateral factor is the ratio of how much you have to supply in order to borrow.
- Another note is you cannot supply and borrow the same token at the same time.

Step 1

- Go the Compound's main page https://app.compound.finance/
- Choose which tokens you wish to borrow on the right bar. I chose USDC

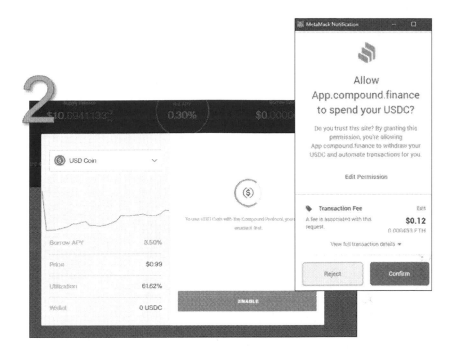

Step 2

- A pop-up on USDC will appear
- First-timers will need to enable it
- Each token has to enable it individually

Step 3
- I punched in the amount of how much I want to borrow. I wanted to borrow 2 USDC
- Confirm the transaction with your wallet

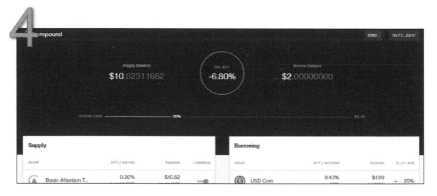

Step 4
- Finished!
- You can see how much you supply and how much you borrow on the main page.

Recommended Readings

1. The DeFi Series – An overview of the ecosystem and major protocols (Alethio) https://medium.com/alethio/the-defi-series-an-overview-of-the-ecosystem-and-major-protocols-da27d7b11191
2. Compound FAQ (Robert Leshner) https://medium.com/compound-finance/faq-1a2636713b69
3. DeFi Series #1 - Decentralized Cryptoasset Lending & Borrowing (Binance Research) https://research.binance.com/analysis/decentralized-finance-lending-borrowing
4. Zero to DeFi – A beginner's guide to earning passive income via Compound Finance (Defi Pulse) https://defipulse.com/blog/zero-to-defi-cdai/
5. I took out a loan with cryptocurrency and didn't sign a thing (Stan Schroeder) https://mashable.com/article/defi-guide-ethereum-decentralized-finance.amp
6. Earn passive income with Compound. (DefiZap) https://defitutorials.substack.com/p/earn-passive-income-with-compound

# CHAPTER 7: DECENTRALIZED EXCHANGES (DEX)

While Centralized Exchanges (CEXs) allow for large trades to happen with plenty of liquidity, it still carries a lot of risks because users do not have ownership of their assets in exchanges. In 2019, over $290 million worth of cryptocurrencies were stolen and over 500,000 login information were leaked from exchanges.[10]

More people are realizing these risks and are turning to Decentralized Exchanges (DEXs). DEXs work by using smart contracts and on-chain transactions to reduce or eliminate the need for an intermediary. Some popular Decentralized Exchanges include projects like Kyber Network, Uniswap, Dex Blue and dYdX.

There are two kinds of DEXs - order book-based DEXs and liquidity pool-based DEXs. Order book DEXs like dYdX and dex.blue operate similarly to CEXs where users can place buy and sell orders at either their chosen limit prices or at market prices. The main difference between the two is that for CEXs, assets for the trade would be held on the exchange wallet whereas for DEXs, assets for trade can be held on users' own wallets.

---

[10] "Most Significant Hacks of 2019 — New Record of Twelve in ...." 5 Jan. 2020, https://cointelegraph.com/news/most-significant-hacks-of-2019-new-record-of-twelve-in-one-year.

However, one of the biggest problems facing order book-based DEXs is liquidity. Users may have to wait a long time for their orders to be filled in the order book. To solve this issue, liquidity pools-based DEXs were introduced. Liquidity pools are essentially reserves of tokens in smart contracts and users can buy or sell tokens instantly from the available tokens in the liquidity pool. The price of the token is determined algorithmically and increases for large trades. DEXs liquidity pools can be shared across multiple DEX platforms and this pushes up the available liquidity on any single platform. Examples of liquidity pools-based DEXs are Kyber Network, Bancor, and Uniswap. We will be going through the Uniswap example in this book.

One of the features offered by CEXs is the margin trading function. Margin trading enables an investor to trade leveraged positions, boosting one's purchasing power to gain potentially higher returns. Innovations to bring margin trading on DEXs have appeared as well. Examples of DEXs offering decentralized margin trading are dYdX, NUO Network and DDEX. In this book, we will be exploring dYdX which combines both decentralized lending and borrowing markets with margin trading on their exchange.

## Uniswap

Uniswap Exchange is a decentralized token exchange protocol built on Ethereum that allows direct swapping of tokens without the need to use a centralized exchange. When using a centralized exchange, you will need to deposit tokens to an exchange, place an order on the order book, and then withdraw the swapped tokens.

On Uniswap, you can simply swap your tokens directly from your wallet without having to go through the three steps above. All you need to do is send your tokens from your wallet to Uniswap's smart contract address and you will receive your desired token in return in your wallet. There is no order book and the token exchange rate is determined algorithmically. All this is achieved via liquidity pools and the automated market maker mechanism.

## Liquidity Pools

Liquidity pools are token reserves that sit on Uniswap's smart contracts and are available for users to exchange tokens with. For example, using ETH-DAI trading pair with 100 ETH and 20,000 DAI in the liquidity reserves, a user that wants to buy ETH using DAI may send 202.02 DAI to the Uniswap smart contract to get 1 ETH in return. Once the swap has taken place, the liquidity pool is left with 99 ETH and 20,202.02 DAI.

Liquidity pools reserves are provided by liquidity providers who are incentivized to obtain a proportionate fee of Uniswap's 0.3% transaction fee. This fee is charged for every token swap on Uniswap.

There are no restrictions and anyone can be a liquidity provider - the only requirement is that one needs to provide ETH and the quoted trading token to be swapped to at the current Uniswap exchange rate. As of Feb 2020, over 125,000 ETH have been locked into Uniswap. The amount of reserves held by a pool plays a huge role in determining how prices are set by the Automated Market Maker Mechanism.

## Automated Market Maker Mechanism

Prices of assets in the pool are algorithmically determined using the Automated Market Maker (AMM) algorithm. AMM works by maintaining a Constant Product based on the amount of liquidity in both sides of the pool.

Let's continue the ETH-DAI liquidity pool example which has 100 ETH and 20,000 DAI. To calculate the Constant Product, Uniswap will multiply both these amounts together.

| ETH liquidity (x) | * | DAI liquidity (y) | = | Constant Product (k) |
|---|---|---|---|---|
| 100 | * | 20,000 | = | 2,000,000 |

Using AMM, at any given time, the Constant Product (k) must always remain at 2,000,000. If someone buys ETH using DAI, ETH will be removed from the liquidity pool while DAI will be added into the liquidity pool.

The price for this ETH will be determined asymptotically. The larger the order, the larger the premium that is charged. Premium refers to the additional amount of DAI required in order to purchase 1 ETH compared to the original price of 200 DAI per ETH.

The table on page 82 further elaborates the asymptotic pricing and the movement of liquidity when orders to purchase ETH are made.

As can be seen from the table, the larger the amount of ETH that a user wishes to buy, the larger the premium that will be charged. This ensures that the liquidity pool will never be out of liquidity.

| ETH Purchased | Cost per ETH in DAI | Total Cost in DAI | Premium | New DAI Liquidity | New ETH liquidity | Product (k) |
|---|---|---|---|---|---|---|
| 1 | 202.02 | 202.02 | 1.01% | 20,202.02 | 99 | 2,000,000 |
| 5 | 210.52 | 1,052.63 | 5.26% | 21,052.63 | 95 | 2,000,000 |
| 10 | 222.22 | 2,222.22 | 11.11% | 22,222.22 | 90 | 2,000,000 |
| 50 | 400 | 20,000 | 200% | 40,000 | 50 | 2,000,000 |
| 75 | 800 | 60,000 | 400% | 80,000 | 25 | 2,000,000 |
| 99 | 20,000 | 1,980,000 | 10,000% | 2,000,000 | 1 | 2,000,000 |
| 100 | Infinity | Infinity | Infinity | Infinity | 0 | 2,000,000 |

## How to get a token added on Uniswap?

Unlike centralized exchanges, Uniswap as a decentralized exchange does not have a team or gatekeepers to evaluate and decide on which tokens to list. Instead, any ERC-20 token can be listed on Uniswap by anyone and be traded as long as liquidity exists for the given pair. All a user needs to do is to interact with the platform to register the new token and a new market will be initialized for this token.

And that's it for Uniswap - if you're keen to get started or test it out, we've included step-by-step guides on how to (i) swap tokens, (ii) provide liquidity and (iii) stop providing liquidity. Otherwise, head on to the next section to read more on the next DeFi app!

## Uniswap: Step-by-Step Guide
Swapping Tokens

Step 1
- Head on over to https://uniswap.io/ and click swap token
- To start using Uniswap, you will need to connect to a wallet. You may connect your Metamask wallet. Connecting your wallet is free, all you need to do is sign a transaction

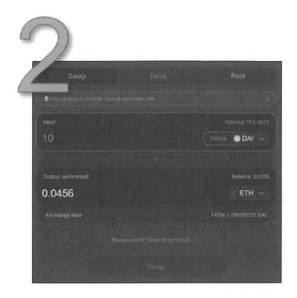

Step 2
- After connecting your wallet, choose which tokens you would like to trade with, in this example, we are using DAI to buy ETH

Step 3
- If it's your first time transacting this token, you'll need to unlock it by paying a small fee
- You'll be prompted with another transaction
- Once your transaction is confirmed, you'll have your ETH!

Provide Liquidity

Step 4

- Go to Pool and fill in the amount of liquidity, you wish to provide. In this case, we're providing 10 DAI worth of liquidity + 0.0461 ETH
- Note: you must have an equivalent amount of ETH to provide liquidity for that token
- After clicking add liquidity, you'll be prompted to sign another transaction
- Once that's done, you're now confirmed as a liquidity provider and stand to earn a proportionate amount of the exchange fees

Stop Providing Liquidity

Step 5

- What if you don't want to provide liquidity anymore?
- Go back to the pool and select remove liquidity
- As you can see, I'll be getting back an extra 0.0417 DAI from only 10 DAI
- Note that the ratio of my ETH and DAI is now different, so that's one of the caveats with liquidity pools, if I had removed it later, I might have a very different proportion of DAI to ETH
- Another thing to note is when removing liquidity, I trade Pool Tokens. Think of it as the proof of how much your share is in the pool. When you remove your liquidity, you will be burning the Pool tokens to get back your DAI and ETH.

## Recommended Readings

1. Getting Started (Uniswap) https://docs.uniswap.io/
2. The Ultimate Guide to Uniswap. (DefiZap) https://defitutorials.substack.com/p/the-ultimate-guide-to-uniswap
3. A Graphical Guide for Understanding Uniswap (EthHub) https://docs.ethhub.io/guides/graphical-guide-for-understanding-uniswap
4. Uniswap — A Unique Exchange (Cyrus Younessi) https://medium.com/scalar-capital/uniswap-a-unique-exchange-f4ef44f807bf
5. What is Uniswap? A Detailed Beginner's Guide (Bisade Asolo) https://www.mycryptopedia.com/what-is-uniswap-a-detailed-beginners-guide/
6. Are Uniswap's Liquidity Pools Right for You? (Chris Blec) https://defiprime.com/uniswap-liquidity-pools
7. Understanding Uniswap Returns (Pintail) https://medium.com/@pintail/understanding-uniswap-returns-cc593f3499ef
8. UniSwap Traction Analysis (Ganesh) https://www.covalenthq.com/blog/understanding-uniswap-data-analysis/
9. A Deep Dive into Liquidity Pools (Rebecca Mqamelo) https://blog.zerion.io/liquidity-pools-8ac8cf8cf230

## dYdX

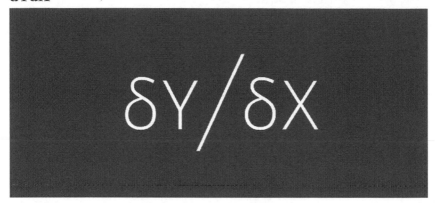

dYdX is a decentralized exchange protocol for lending, borrowing and margin/leveraged trading. It currently supports 3 assets—ETH, USDC, and DAI. Through the use of off-chain order books with on-chain settlements, the dYdX protocol aims to create efficient, fair and trustless financial markets not governed by any central authority.

At first glance, dYdX appears to have some similarities to Compound - users can supply assets (lend) to earn interest and also loan assets (borrow) after depositing collateral. However, dYdX takes it one step further by incorporating a margin and leveraged exchange with ETH margin trading up to 5X leverage using either DAI or USDC.

## Lending

| ASSET | PRICE | INTEREST RATE (APR) |
|---|---|---|
| ◆ ETH | $280.89 | Earn 0.02% / Pay 0.39% |
| Ⓢ USDC | $1.00 | Earn 6.06% / Pay 7.07% |
| ⊜ DAI | $1.00 | Earn 8.35% / Pay 9.29% |

If you are a crypto holder who would like to generate some passive income on your otherwise unproductive cryptoassets, you may consider lending it out on dYdX for some yield. It is relatively low risk and by depositing it into dYdX, interest accrues every second without any additional maintenance or management needed. As a lender on dYdX, you only need to be mindful of the earned Interest Rate (APR) - this represents how much you will earn from lending out your assets.

## Who pays the interest for my deposit?

The interest you earn is paid by other users who are borrowing the same asset. dYdX only allows for over-collateralized loans. This means that borrowers must always have enough collateral to pay back their loaned amount. If a borrower's collateral falls below the 115% collateral ratio threshold (i.e < $115 of ETH for $100 DAI loan), their collateral is automatically sold until they fully cover their position.

Interest rates are dynamic and change over time based on supply and demand, ensuring that users will always earn market rates. Additionally, both the initial capital and interest earned can be deposited and withdrawn at any time.

## Borrowing

You can use dYdX to borrow any of the supported assets (ETH, DAI and USDC) as long as a 1.25x initial / 1.15x minimum collateral ratio is maintained. Borrowed funds are deposited directly to your wallet and can be freely transferred, exchanged or traded.

As a borrower on dYdX, the two numbers you need to look out for are:
(i) **Interest Rate (APR)** - how much you pay to loan the money
(ii) **Account collateralization ratio** - This is the ratio of your asset / loan amount. You can borrow until this ratio is 125%, and you will be liquidated once it falls below 115%.

## Margin & Leveraged Trading

*Trade Page*

In dYdX you can enter either short or long positions with leverages up to 5x. When margin trading on dYdX, funds are automatically borrowed from lenders on the platform.

Consider a scenario where you start with 300 DAI & 0 ETH in your dYdX account. If you are going to short ETH (assume ETH is now $150), you will:

1. Take a loan of 1 ETH ($150)
2. Sell loaned ETH for 150 DAI, balance in dYdX is now 450 DAI & -1 ETH
3. Assuming ETH price goes to $100, you can now rebuy 1 ETH for $100 to repay your debt.
4. Your final balance is 350 DAI—you profit 50 DAI ($50)

With dYdX, you don't need to actually own ETH to enter a short position. You can borrow it and enter a short position it all in one place.

*Pro Tip:*
*Collateral used to secure margin trades continuously earns interest, meaning you don't have to worry about losing out on interest when waiting for an order to fill. This feature is unique to dYdX as far as we know as of the time of writing.*

## What is leverage?

Consider two different leveraged positions scenarios (numbers approximated) for a trader who has 10 ETH ($150 per ETH), or $1500. In the first scenario, the trader enters a **5x long position with 1 ETH ($150):**
  a. The position size would be 5 ETH ($750)
  b. 10% of the Portfolio is at risk (1/10 ETH used)
  c. A price movement of ~10% ($15 on ETH) downwards will liquidate the trader's position, meaning there is very little buffer for price spikes.

On the other hand, if the trader enters a **2x long position with 1 ETH ($150):**
  a. The position size would be 2 ETH ($300)
  b. 10% of the portfolio is at risk (1/10 ETH used)
  c. A price movement of ~45% ($65 on ETH) downwards will liquidate the trader's position.

Essentially, leverage is really just a factor of how much risk a trader wants to take (in terms of exposure to price movements), which in turn determines a trader's distance to liquidation. High risk, high rewards!

*Note: Margin positions for trades made from the US are limited to 28 days as of Feb 2020.*

## What is liquidation?

On dYdX, whenever a position falls below the collateral threshold of 115%, any existing borrows will be deemed as risky and in order to protect lenders, risky positions are liquidated. Collaterals backing the borrows will be sold until negative balances are 0, along with a liquidation fee of 5%.

## How are Profits/losses calculated?

For example, you open a 5x long with a 3 ETH deposit with an open price of $220.

You'll need to borrow $220*12 = 2640 DAI to buy 12 additional ETH (Total of 15 ETH locked in your position)

If you close the position at 250, you'll need to pay back your loan of 2640 DAI with

= 2640/250 ETH

= 10.56 ETH

This will leave you with 15 - 10.56 = 4.44 ETH. So your profit would be 4.44-3 = 1.44 ETH

Steps to calculate profit:
1. Determine initial leverage and deposit amount to get position size (Leverage*Deposit)
2. Loan Amount = (Position Size - Deposit) * Open Price
3. Loan to pay back = Loan Amount/Closing Price
4. Balance = Position Size - Loan to Pay back
5. Profit = Balance - Initial Deposit

And that's it for dYdX—if you're keen to get started or test it out, we've included step-by-step guides on how to (i) lend to earn interest, (ii) borrow and (iii) margin/leverage trade. Otherwise, head on to the next section to read more on the next DeFi app!

## dYdX: Step-by-Step Guide

Step 1
- Go to https://dydx.exchange/
- Click "START TRADING"
- Click connect wallet on the sidebar

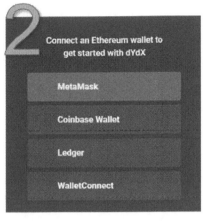

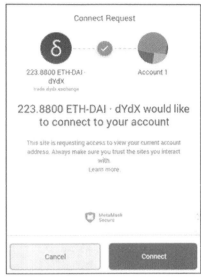

## Step 2

- Choose which wallet to connect

## Step 3

- You have no balance in your dYdX account

- Click "Deposit"
- If you are a first-timer, you will need to enable the token you wish to deposit. In this case, I wish to deposit DAI

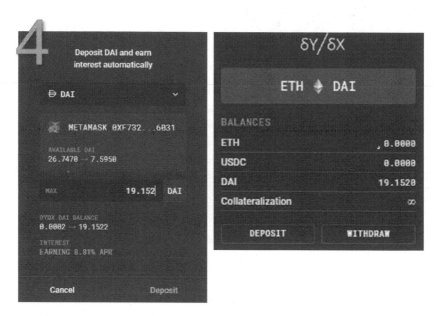

Step 4

- Enter the amount of DAI you wish to deposit and proceed
- You will see the balance upon confirmed transaction

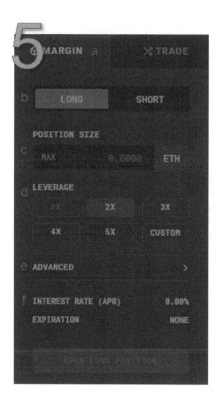

Step 5
- Now you can start trading!
- Here is a little guidance:
  a. You can trade Margin or a normal spot trading.
     Margin will incur interest because you are trading on borrowed funds
  b. This is the position you could take "long" or "short"
  c. Position size is how much you wish to purchase to trade
  d. This is the size of your borrowing. If your dYdX has 1 ETH, you could borrow up to 5X (now your position size should be up to 5 ETH)
  e. This is where you would fix how much slippage you allow to happen for your position price
  f. How much interest will incur you depending on the size of your margin (borrowing)

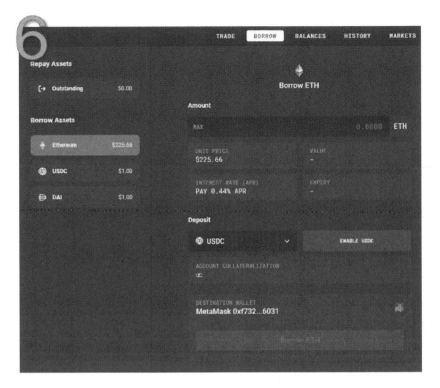

Step 6
- Alternatively, you could borrow ETH, USDC and DAI
- You will have to put up collateral before you can borrow
- You will need to enable the coin before you could start borrowing

## Recommended Readings

1. dYdX Exchange Review http://defipicks.com/2019/11/23/dydx-exchange-review/
2. Margin Trading on Centralized vs. Decentralized Exchanges (Syed Shoeb) https://medium.com/nuo-news/why-you-should-choose-decentralized-margin-trading-over-centralized-e309e61e6e72
3. Liquidators: The Secret Whales Helping DeFi Function https://medium.com/dragonfly-research/liquidators-the-secret-whales-helping-defi-function-acf132fbea5e

# CHAPTER 8: DECENTRALIZED DERIVATIVES

A derivative is a contract whose value is derived from another underlying asset such as stocks, commodities, currencies, indexes, bonds, or interest rates. There are several types of derivatives such as futures, options, and swaps. Each type of derivative serves a different purpose and different investors buy or sell them for different reasons.

Some of the reasons investors trade derivatives are: to hedge themself against the volatility of the underlying asset, speculate on the directional movement of the underlying asset or leverage their holdings. Derivatives are extremely risky in nature and one must be equipped with strong financial knowledge and strategies when trading them.

The Total Value Locked in DeFi derivatives Dapps is $114.3 million or 12% of the DeFi ecosystem[11]. Though the figure is relatively low compared to other DeFi markets such as the lending market ($745.6 million), it is worth noting the decentralized derivative market has only been around for one year and it has grown significantly. Some of the major DeFi derivatives Protocols are Synthetix and bZx.

In this book, we will deep dive into Synthetix, the biggest DeFi derivative protocol.

---

[11] "DeFi Pulse." https://defipulse.com/.

## Synthetix

Synthetix is exactly as the name sounds, a protocol for Synthetic Assets (called Synths) on Ethereum. There are two parts to Synthetix - Synthetic Assets (**Synths**) and its exchange, **Synthetix.Exchange**. Synthetix allows for the issuance and trading of Synths.

### What are Synthetic Assets (Synths)?
Synths are assets or a mixture of assets that have the same value or effect as another asset. Synths track the value of underlying assets and allow exposure to the assets without the need to hold the actual asset.

There are currently two different types of Synths - Normal Synths and Inverse Synths. Normal Synths are positively correlated with the underlying assets while Inverse Synths are negatively correlated to the underlying assets.

An example of a Synthetic Asset is Synthetic Gold (sXAU) which tracks the price performance of gold. Synthetix tracks real-world asset prices by utilizing the services of Chainlink, a smart contract oracle that obtains price feed from several trusted third party sources to prevent tampering.

An example of an Inverse Synthetic Asset is Inverse Bitcoin (iBTC) which tracks the inverse price performance of Bitcoin. There are 3 key values related to each Inverse Synths—the entry price, lower limit, and upper limit.

Let's consider Inverse Synthetic Bitcoin (iBTC) as an example. Assume that at the time of creation, Bitcoin (BTC) is priced at $10,600 - this will be the entry price. If Bitcoin moves down $400 to $10,200, the iBTC Synth will now be worth an additional $400 and will be priced at $11,000. The opposite will also be true. If Bitcoin moves up to $11,000, the iBTC Synth will now be worth $10,200.

Inverse Synths trade in a range with a 50% upper and lower limit from the entry price. This places a cap to the maximum profit or loss you can obtain on Inverse Synths. Once either of the limits is reached, the tokens' exchange rates are frozen and the positions liquidated. Once disabled and liquidated, these Inverse Synths can only be exchanged at Synthetix.Exchange at those fixed values. They are then reset with different limits.

## Why Synthetic Assets?

As mentioned above, Synths give traders price exposure to the asset without the need to actually hold the underlying asset. Compared to traditional gold brokerages, Synthetic Gold (sXAU) allows traders to participate in the market with much less hassle (no sign-ups, no traveling, no middleman etc.).

Synths have another utility—they can be traded frictionlessly between one another, meaning Synthetic Gold can be switched for Synthetic JPY, Synthetic Silver or Synthetic Bitcoin easily on Synthetix.Exchange. This also means that anyone with an Ethereum wallet now has open access to any real-world asset!

## How are Synths Created?

The idea behind the creation of Synths is similar to the creation of DAI on Maker. You have to first stake ETH as collateral on Maker's smart contract before being allowed to create DAI based on the collateral posted.

For Synths, you first need to stake the Synthetix Network Token (SNX), which acts as the collateral backing the entire system. SNX is less liquid compared to ETH and its price is generally more volatile. To counter that, a large minimum initial collateral of 750% is needed on Synthetic compared to the minimum 150% initial collateral needed on Maker.

This means that to mint $100 worth of Synthetic USD (sUSD), you will need a minimum of $750 worth of SNX as collateral.

Note: As of 27 November 2019, the only Synth that can be minted by users is sUSD[12].

Minting of Synths is a fairly intricate system. It entails the staker taking on debt, the levels of which are dynamically changed depending on the total value of Synths in the global debt pool, causing the debt owed by the staker to fluctuate with changing values. For example, if 100% of the Synths in the system were synthetic Ethereum (sETH), and the price doubles, everyone's debt would double including the staker's own debt as well.

Once minted, these Synths tokens can be traded on Synthetix Exchange or on Decentralized Exchanges like Uniswap.

*If you want to trade Synths but don't want to take on Debt or mint your own Synths, you can actually buy it on the sETH Uniswap Pool. The sETH pool on Uniswap is currently the largest Pool on Uniswap with over 35,000 ETH (~$80mm @ $200 ETH) in liquidity).*

## What Assets do Synths Support?
At the point of writing, Synths support the following 4 major asset classes (full list: https://www.synthetix.io/tokens):
  (i) **Cryptocurrencies:** Ethereum (ETH), Bitcoin (BTC), Binance Coin (BNB), Tezos (XTZ), Maker (MKR), Tron (TRX), Litecoin (LTC), and Chainlink (LINK)
  (ii) **Commodities:** Gold (XAU) and Silver (XAG)
  (iii) **Fiat Currencies:** USD, AUD, CHF, JPY, EUR, and GBP
  (iv) **Indexes:** CEX and DEFI

## Index Synths
One of the interesting Synths available on Synthetix is the Index Synths. At the time of writing, there are 2 different Index Synths, namely sCEX and sDEFI.

---

[12] "The Vega Release - Synthetix Blog." 27 Nov. 2019,
   https://blog.synthetix.io/the-vega-release/.

Index Synths provide traders with exposure to a basket of tokens without the need to purchase all the tokens. The index will mirror the overall performance of the underlying tokens. Index Synths allow for exposure to particular segments of the industry as well as diversification of risks without the need to actually hold and manage various tokens.

## sCEX

sCEX is an Index Synth designed to give traders exposure to a basket of Centralized Exchange (CEX) tokens roughly approximating their weighted market capitalization. The current sCEX index consists of Binance Coin (BNB), Bitfinex's LEO Token (LEO), Huobi Token (HT), OKEx Token (OKB) and KuCoin Shares (KCS).

There is also the Inverse Synth called iCEX which is an inverse of the sCEX Index Synth and works like other Inverse Synths.

## sDEFI

With the growing interest in DeFi, the sDEFI Index Synth was introduced to provide traders with an index exposure to a basket of DeFi utility tokens in the ecosystem. The current sDEFI index consists of the following tokens: Chainlink (LINK), Maker (MKR), 0x (ZRX), Synthetix Network Token (SNX), REN (REN), Loopring (LRC), Kyber Network (KNC), Bancor Network Token (BNT), and Melon (MLN).

The inverse of this Index Synth is called iDEFI.

## Fun fact:

These Index Synths were created through a series of Twitter polls. The weight of each token was determined using the proportionate market capitalization of each token, before being amended as per community feedback.

## Synthetix Exchange

Synthetix.Exchange is a decentralized exchange platform designed for the trading of SNX and Synths without orders books employed by most DEXs. That is, rather than a peer-to-peer system (Uniswap or dYdX) which relies on users to supply liquidity, Synthetix.Exchange allows users to trade directly against a contract that maintains constantly adequate liquidity, thus theoretically reducing risks of slippage or lack of liquidity.

Since users are purchasing a synthetic contract rather than trading the underlying asset, users are able to buy up to the total amount of collateral in the system without having any effect on the contract's price. For example, a $10,000,000 BTC buy/sell order would likely result in considerable slippage in traditional exchanges, but not in Synthetix Exchange as users trade against the Synthetix contract directly.

The other thing to know about Synthetix is that over 2020 they'll be launching a range of new trading features, including such new assets as synthetic indices and equities, leveraged trading, binary options, synthetic futures, and triggered orders.

And that's it for Synthetix - if you are keen to get started or test it out, we have included a step-by-step guide on how to mint a Synth. Otherwise, head on to the next section to read more on the next DeFi app!

## Synthetix: Step-by-Step Guide

Step 1
- Before you could mint any synth, you will need SNX token to be used as collateral
- If you do not have one, you could check out our SNX page (https://www.coingecko.com/en/coins/synthetix-network-token#markets) to see the list of available exchanges to trade for it

- In this tutorial, we swap our ETH for SNX on Uniswap (https://uniswap.exchange/swap)
- Connect your wallet and enter the amount of ETH you wish to swap for SNX

## Step 2

- To mint your Synth, go to https://mintr.synthetix.io/
- Connect your wallet

## Step 3

- Once you are on the page, click on "Mint"

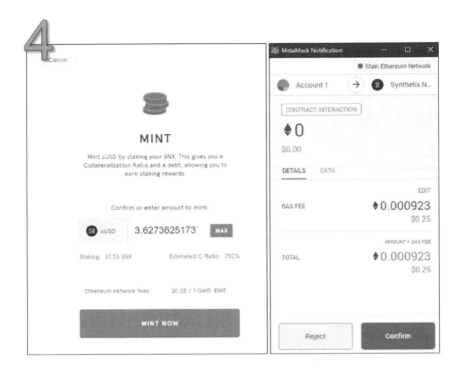

Step 4

- Enter the amount you wish to mint. Here I put max
- Note: The available amount to mint depends on the collateral ratio SNX to the Synth
- Current collateral ratio is 750%
- So $27.21/750\% \approx 3.63$ sUSD
- If you are a first-timer, you will need to enable it first before continuing with the transaction

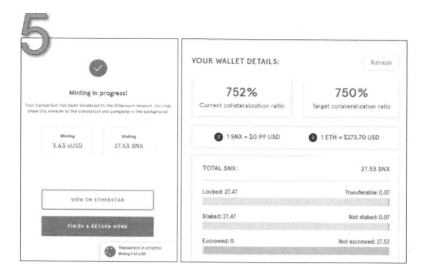

Step 5

- After confirmation, you will be able to see your wallet balance as shown above.

**Recommended Readings**

1. Crypto Derivatives, Lending, and a touch of Stablecoin (Gary Basin) https://blockgeeks.com/guides/defi-use-cases-the-best-examples-of-decentralised-finance/#_Tool_2_DeFi_Derivatives

2. DeFi Use cases: The Best Examples of Decentralised Finance (Rajarshi Mitra) https://hackernoon.com/crypto-derivatives-lending-and-a-touch-of-stablecoin-59e727510024

3. The Ultimate Guide To Synthetix. (DefiZap and @DegenSpartan) https://defitutorials.substack.com/p/the-ultimate-guide-to-synthetix

4. Synthetix (Cooper Turley and Lucas Campbell) https://fitznerblockchain.consulting/synthetix/

5. Synthetix for dummies (TwiceCrypto) https://medium.com/@TwiceCrypto/synthetix-for-dummies-477a0760d335

6. Synthetic Instruments In DeFi : Synthetix (Joel John) https://www.decentralised.co/understanding-synthetix/amp/?

7. Synthetic Assets in DeFi: Use Cases & Opportunities (Dmitriy Berenzon) https://medium.com/zenith-ventures/synthetic-assets-in-defi-use-cases-opportunities-19b11f57a776

8. The Value and Risk of Synthetix (Gavin Low) https://medium.com/the-spartan-group/the-value-and-risk-of-synthetix-45204346ce

# CHAPTER 9: DECENTRALIZED FUND MANAGEMENT

Fund management is the process of overseeing your assets and managing its cash flow to generate a return on your investments. We have started seeing innovative DeFi teams starting to build ways for users to better manage their funds in a decentralized manner.

In DeFi, fund management is conducted in a manner where it removes the investment manager and lets you choose the asset management strategy that best suits your financial need. The decentralized fund management also reduces the fees paid.

The Dapp will have algorithms to conduct trades for you automatically instead of doing it yourself. To understand how fund management can work in the decentralized ledger, we will introduce you to Token Sets.

## TokenSets

TokenSets is a platform that allows crypto users to buy Strategy Enabled Tokens (SET). These tokens have automated asset management strategies that allow you to easily manage your cryptocurrency portfolio without the need to manually execute the trading strategy. With an automated trading strategy, you will not need to manually monitor the market 24/7, thus reducing missed opportunities and risks from emotional trading.

Each Set is an ERC20 token consisting of a basket of cryptocurrencies that automatically rebalances its holdings based on the strategy that you choose. In other words, SET essentially implements cryptocurrency trading strategies in the form of tokens.

### What kinds of Sets are there?
There are two kinds of Sets: (i) Robo Sets and (ii) Social Trading Sets.

### Robo Sets
Robo Sets are algorithmic trading strategies that buys and sells tokens based on predefined rules encoded in smart contracts. There are currently 4 main types of algorithmic strategies, namely:

(i) **Buy and Hold:** This strategy realigns the portfolio to its target allocation to prevent overexposure to any one token and spreads the risk over other tokens.
(ii) **Trend Trading:** This strategy uses Technical Analysis indicators to shift from target asset to stablecoins based on the implemented strategy.
(iii) **Range-Bound:** This strategy automates buying and selling within a designated range and is only intended for bearish or neutral markets.

(iv) **Inverse:** This strategy is meant for those who wish to "short" a benchmark. Traders can purchase this when they think a benchmark is due for a correction.

## Social Trading Sets

Social Trading Sets enable users to follow top trading strategies by some featured traders on TokenSets. By buying this Social Trading Set, you can copy the trades performed by these featured traders automatically. Social Trading Sets are also algorithmic-based, but instead of it being written by the TokenSets team such as those found in Robo Sets, they are written by prominent traders.

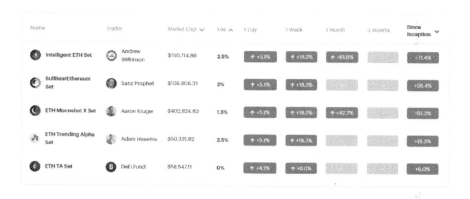

## How are Sets helpful?

Sets essentially tokenize trading strategies. If you are keen to try out any of the selected trading strategies or follow professional traders' footsteps, Set is likely the easiest way to go about it.

That being said, always do your due diligence. Just because a Set has been performing well historically does not mean that it will continue to do so. The cryptocurrency market is highly volatile and the old saying of "past performance is not an indicator of future results" is especially true here. Instead, research and compare the available strategies to see which one makes the most sense to you and then use TokenSets to get started in no time.

We will be going through one of the best performing Robo Set as an example—the ETH/BTC RSI Ratio Trading Set. In this case, the Robo Set follows the Trend Trading Strategy which uses the Relative Strength Index (RSI) technical indicator. This trading strategy saw the value increase of 102.33% versus 41.29% for holding BTC or 94.17% for holding ETH. Since Token Set is relatively new, there is only performance data for the past 3 months as of writing time.

That's it for TokenSets—if you are keen to get started or test it out, we have included a step-by-step guide on how to start getting Sets. Otherwise, head on to the next section to read more on the next DeFi app!

## TokenSets: Step-by-Step Guide

Step 1
- Go to https://www.tokensets.com/
- Click "Get Started"
- Continue Click "Next" until a request to your wallet pops out
- Click "Connect" to connect your wallet

Step 2
- Accept Terms of Services and Privacy Policy
- It is optional to add your email

Step 3

- Scroll down and you are able to see there are two kinds of Sets:

    **1. Social Trading Sets**

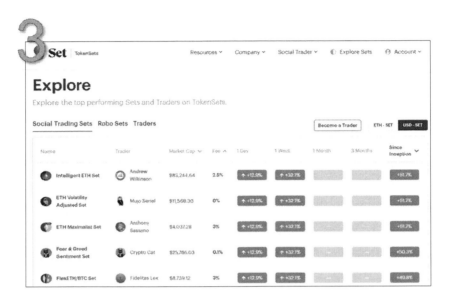

## 2. Robo Sets

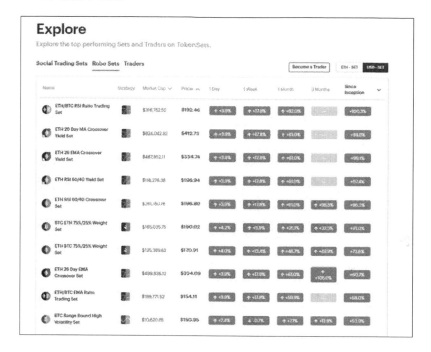

- You could choose which sets you wish to buy
- Note: You should do your own due diligence and research on which sets to purchase!

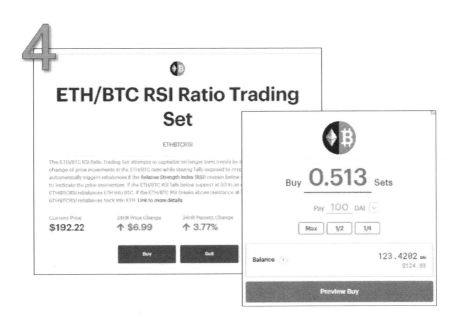

Step 4
- I chose Robo Sets
- Click on the Name "ETH/BTC RSI Ratio Trading Set"
- Click "Buy"
- Enter the amount of sets you wish to buy

Step 5

- For first-timer, you have to enable Dai before trading
- After confirmed approval, you are able to continue with your purchase

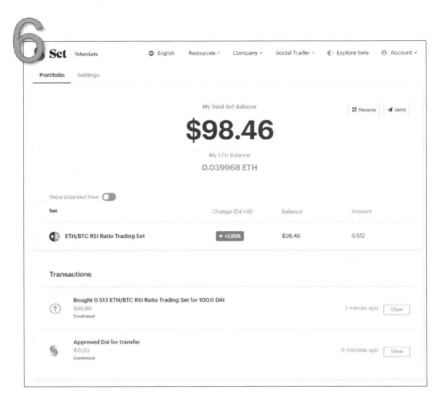

Step 6
- Done!

## Recommended Readings

1. Automated Asset Management with Set Protocol. (DefiZap)
   https://defitutorials.substack.com/p/automated-asset-management-with-set
2. DeFi10 Part 1: Lessons in Building a DeFi Portfolio
   https://thedefiant.substack.com/p/defi10-part-1-lessons-in-building
3. DeFi10 Part2: Becoming a Programmable Money Fund Manager
   https://thedefiant.substack.com/p/defi10-part2-becoming-a-programmable
4. Returns of Hodling versus DeFi-ing (Evgeny Yurtaev)
   https://blog.zerion.io/returns-of-holding-vs-defi-ing-c6f050e89c8e

# CHAPTER 10: DECENTRALIZED LOTTERY

Thus far, we have gone through various protocols for stablecoins, decentralized exchanges, swaps, and derivatives - all of them serious stuff. In this section we will introduce you to something light and fun - a decentralized, no-loss lottery.

Earlier in February 2020, a user who had deposited only $10 won $1,648 in PoolTogether's weekly Dai Prize Pool, a 1 in 69,738 chance of winning. The best part of PoolTogether's lottery is that participants are able to get a refund of the $10 deposit if he or she did not actually win. There is no loser in this game, but only opportunity cost involved. Read on to find out more.

## PoolTogether

### What is PoolTogether?

PoolTogether is a decentralized no-loss lottery or decentralized prize savings application where users get to keep their initial deposit amount after the lottery prize is drawn. Instead of funding the prize money using the lottery tickets purchased, the prize money is funded using the interest earned on Compound by the pooled user deposits. For each round of PoolTogether, all the user deposits will be sent to Compound to earn an interest and one lucky winner will be selected at random at the end of each interval to win the entire interest prize money.

Participating in PoolTogether is fairly straightforward - simply "purchase" PoolTogether tickets using DAI or USDC. Each ticket represents 1 entry and the chance of winning increases proportionately with the number of tickets purchased. PoolTogether currently supports 2 different lotteries - a weekly DAI pool (launched December 2019) and a daily USDC pool (launched February 2020).

A portion of the money currently earning interest in PoolTogether is sponsored. Currently, this amounts to roughly $250,000 in the Dai pool and $200,000 in the USDC pool. This is provided by sponsors to increase the interest earned on Compound each week to make the prize pool larger. The sponsored tickets are not eligible to be a winner on PoolTogether.

This concept is not new and it is similar to Prize-Linked Savings Account (PLSA) where it incentivizes people to save more in their bank's savings account by providing sweepstakes for lucky winners. PLSA is a popular concept with banks and credit unions from many countries around the world offering such programs. One of the known PLSA programs is "Save to Win" by Michigan Credit Union League[13].

## Why bother with Decentralized Lotteries?

One of the attractions of decentralized lotteries in the context of PoolTogether is that funds do not go through middleman or brokers, but are instead held by smart contracts that have been audited (https://www.pooltogether.com/audits). There is also no lock-up period on funds, meaning that they can be withdrawn at any moment.

Traditionally, the jurisdiction and protection laws of the gambling industry have made real-world no-loss lottery, such as PLSA programs, restrictive to users from certain geographical areas to join. This is where Decentralized Applications truly shine as well - anyone from anywhere can participate if they have the funds to do so.

## What's the Catch?

Surely there can't be free money? Spot on! There's a small catch - the opportunity cost of putting your funds into PoolTogether. If you put your funds into Compound to supply liquidity, you will be able to earn interest from it but if you put it into PoolTogether, you will lose the interest that can be earned from Compound but instead now have the opportunity to win the lottery. Your "fee" to enter the lottery is effectively whatever interest you would have earned by lending it out on Compound.

## So, Lending on Compound vs. participating in PoolTogether?

Naturally, the next question we asked ourselves - would it be better to put our money in Compound or in PoolTogether? We geeked out on some numbers - check out the table below for a comparison:

---

[13] "What Are Prize-Linked Savings Accounts? – The Balance." 21 Feb. 2019, https://www.thebalance.com/what-are-prize-linked-savings-accounts-4587608.

| Weekly PoolTogether (DAI) | |
|---|---|
| **Currently in PoolTogether** | |
| Total Amount | 999,000.00 |
| *Where* | |
| Eligible Tickets | 749,000.00 |
| Sponsored | 250,000.00 |
| Open tickets | - |
| **Additional 1,000 Dai** | |
| + Additional Deposit (Dai) | 1,000.00 |
| Compound Supply APR^ | 8.81% |
| Weekly Interest Rate | 0.17% |
| Weekly Interest Earned (Dai) | 1.69 |
| **Updated Figure PoolTogether** | |
| New Total Amount | 1,000,000.00 |
| *where* | |
| New Eligible Tickets | 750,000.00 |
| Sponsored | 250,000.00 |
| Open Tickets | - |
| Prize Pool | 1,694.23 |
| **Analysis** | |
| Chances of Winning Each Time | 0.13% |
| Expected PT Interest in a week | 2.26 |
| Annualised Compound Return | 88.10 |
| Annualised PT Return | 117.47 |
| Annualised PT Expected Return Ratio | 11.75% |
| ALPHA | 1.33 |

| Daily PoolTogether (USDC) | |
|---|---|
| **Currently in PoolTogether** | |
| Total Amount | 299,000.00 |
| *Where* | |
| Eligible Tickets | 99,000.00 |
| Sponsored | 200,000.00 |
| Open tickets | - |
| **Additional 1,000 USDC** | |
| + Additional Deposit (USDC) | 1,000.00 |
| Compound Supply APR^ | 4.84% |
| Daily Interest Rate | 0.01% |
| Weekly Interest Earned (Dai) | 0.13 |
| **Updated Figure PoolTogether** | |
| New Total Amount | 300,000.00 |
| *where* | |
| New Eligible Tickets | 100,000.00 |
| Sponsored | 200,000.00 |
| Open Tickets | - |
| Prize Pool | 39.78 |
| **Analysis** | |
| Chances of Winning Each Time | 1.00% |
| Expected PT Interest in a Day | 0.40 |
| Annualised Compound Return | 48.40 |
| Annualised PT Return | 145.20 |
| Annualised PT Expected Return Ratio | 14.52% |
| ALPHA | 3.00 |

*(Some figures are extracted from https://www.pooltogether.com/#stats and https://compound.finance/markets)*

*tl;dr — at the time of writing PoolTogether seems likelier to have better returns than saving in Compound due to the presence of sponsored tickets that are not eligible to win. But then again, you may not want to compare lotteries with savings so do take our findings with a grain of salt!*

To make better sense of these numbers, we will walk through them line by line. We will start off by assuming that we will be depositing $1,000 worth of either DAI or USDC. Note that the figures given here are just for the purpose of this explanation. For the latest figures, please head over to: https://www.pooltogether.com/#stats

First we will see what the supply APR for Compound is, which you can find here: https://compound.finance/markets. From this rate, we simply divide it by 52 (for weekly) or 365 (for daily) to get the new periodic rates. This would give us the daily and weekly interest earned.

Daily Interest Earned     =    Compound Supply APR/365

Weekly Interest Earned     =    Compound Supply APR/52

Now, since we have the Compound interest amount (which is guaranteed), let's see how much we can expect to win from Pool Together. Let's say the DAI pool has 1,000,000 total tickets while the USDC pool has 300,000 total tickets.

As mentioned earlier, both sponsored and open tickets **WILL NOT** win the lottery. However, they will both contribute to the interest earned for that period, making the prize pool much larger and attracting more people. We then calculate this prize pool amount by simply multiplying the total number of tickets by the weekly/daily interest rate that we calculated earlier.

USDC Prize Pool Amount   =   Total Ticket * Daily Interest Rate

DAI Prize Pool Amount   =   Total Ticket * Weekly Interest Rate

The chance of winning is proportional - the more tickets you buy, the higher the chance of winning. Multiply this with the new interest amount and you'll have Expected Returns for that time frame. Annualize this number and you can compare it to the earlier number from lending it directly to Compound.

Expected Returns   =   $\dfrac{number\ of\ tickets\ owned}{number\ of\ eligible\ tickets} *$ Prize Pool

Annualized Pool Together Returns   =   Expected Returns * Number of Periods (52 or 365)

If this **expected** return is more than good enough for you, do look into getting into it. The Alpha (Expected PoolTogether Returns over Compound lending returns) will decrease as more tickets come into play due to opportunity cost. While the numbers do seem to suggest that it's a good idea to consider PoolTogether, due note that you may be unlucky and not win a single lottery at all throughout a year.

In terms of security and funding, PoolTogether was funded by Maker and has gone through several security audits to review their codes.

PoolTogether also had a fundraising round which enabled them to increase the sponsored pool, and no longer takes fees from the winnings as initially planned, which means more money for the winner![14]

If you're keen to get started or test it out, we've included a step-by-step guide on how to join PoolTogether. Otherwise, head on to the next section to read more on the next DeFi app.

## PoolTogether: Step-by-Step Guide

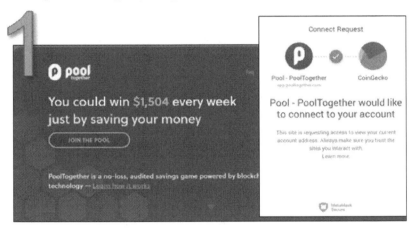

Step 1
- Go to https://www.pooltogether.com/
- Connect your wallet Make sure you have DAI

[14] "PoolTogether raises $1 Million to Expand Prize Linked ...." 3 Feb. 2020, https://medium.com/pooltogether/pooltogether-raises-1-million-to-expand-prize-linked-savings-protocol-eb51a1f88ed8.

Step 2
- Insert the number of tickets you wish to purchase
- *Note: 1 ticket costs 1 DAI and represents 1 entry. Your probability to win goes up with more entries*

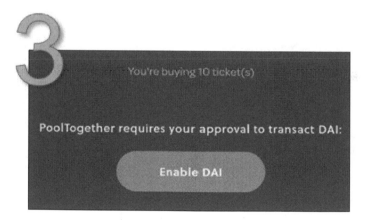

Step 3
- First-time buyer will need to enable DAI

Step 4
- You continue with the purchase afterward

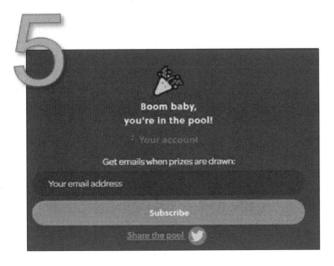

Step 5
- DONE! Just wait for PoolTogether to announce the winner every week

## Recommended Readings

1.  A Simple Explanation of Risks Using PoolTogether (PoolTogether) https://medium.com/pooltogether/a-simple-explanation-of-risks-using-pooltogether-fdf6fecd3864
2.  How PoolTogether Selects Winners https://medium.com/pooltogether/how-pooltogether-selects-winners-9301f8d76730
3.  No Loss Lottery Now Holds $1 Million Tokenized Dollars (TrustNodes) https://www.trustnodes.com/2020/01/29/no-loss-lottery-now-holds-1-million-tokenized-dollars
4.  PoolTogether - Prize Linked Savings Account (Nick Sawinyh) https://defiprime.com/pooltogether
5.  How PoolTogether Turns Saving Money Into a Game (Binance) https://www.binance.vision/tutorials/how-pool-together-turns-saving-money-into-a-game
6.  Leighton Cusack Explains How PoolTogether, a No-Loss Lottery Works - Ep. 6 (CoinGecko Podcast) https://podcast.coingecko.com/719703/2879608-leighton-cusack-explains-how-pooltogether-a-no-loss-lottery-works-ep-6
7.  A data-driven look inside Pool Together (TokenAnalyst) https://research.tokenanalyst.io/a-look-inside-pool-together/

# CHAPTER 11: DECENTRALIZED PAYMENTS

While decentralized payments can already be done by sending ETH or DAI directly, it can still be made better—think cheaper & faster transactions, timed transfers, transfer by conditions as well as standardized invoicing formats and more. Some of the more well-known projects working on decentralized payments are Lighting Network, Request Network, xDai and Sablier.

In this chapter, we will be exploring Sablier—a project which we find interesting and has the potential to solve some of the outstanding issues for people who are vulnerable in society.

## Sablier

### What is Sablier?

Sablier is a payment streaming application—meaning that it allows payment and withdrawals to be made in real time and in small increments (by the second!) between different parties. Think about payments for hourly consultation work, daily contract workers or monthly rent payment made in real time as work/progress is being made. Just like you can stream music on Spotify, so you can stream money on Sablier!

**What Does Streaming Payment Mean?**
Instead of having to wait for a fixed period of time (eg. monthly, bi-weekly) for pay, payments are sent in real time in periods defined and agreed upon by both parties. Through Sablier, payees can now receive their pay in real time and withdraw it whenever they want to.

**Why is this important?**
We think that Sablier has the potential to help those who live paycheck to paycheck. These people are those most vulnerable to delays in their income, where even a few days of delay would mean that they do not have the means to put food on the table.

And when that happens, they often resort to payday loans—a short term, uncollateralized loans with very high interest rates (up to 500% APR[15]). With astronomical interest rates and limited income, payday loan lenders are especially susceptible to debt spirals—one that has seen many arrested in the US for being unable to repay their loan[16].

Trust
Streamed payment can be especially useful for new, remote contract workers who prior to this had to trust their new employers to actually pay them for the work they do. When a contract is signed through Sablier, both parties know for sure that payments are being made and can verify it in real time.

Timing
Traditionally salary payments are made on a monthly or bi-weekly basis but there may be instances where funds are required immediately - and payment

---

[15] "Payday Loans: Disadvantages & Alternatives – Debt.org."
https://www.debt.org/credit/payday-lenders/.
[16] "People are arrested after falling behind on payday loans." 23 Feb. 2020,
https://www.cnbc.com/2020/02/22/people-are-arrested-after-falling-behind-on-payday-loans.html. Accessed 24 Feb. 2020.

streaming can help with this. A salaried employee does not have to wait till payday to access his remuneration - he can withdraw as much as he has earned till date, which may resolve immediate concerns. Furthermore, this is also helpful to avoid delays. Even if a worker fully trusts their employer, streaming paychecks guarantees that the payout will be made in full at the end of the period!

## Example of how it works

Imagine you provide online consultancy services for a fee of $60 per hour ($1 per minute), to begin with you'll likely have to think about whether to:

1. Collect payment upfront, however this may be off-putting to some new clients OR
2. Collect payment later, meaning you'll have to trust your client to pay you OR
3. Use an escrow service/platform to protect both sides for a commission.

With the advent of payment streaming however, you'll no longer need to trust either party to be honest. You can be paid on a minutely basis to ensure that you and your clients both get their money's worth, and that if they do try to run away from paying, you'll lose only 1 minute of your time. Essentially, the "trust" part of an online transaction has been shifted from a person to lines of immutable codes (the blockchain & smart contract).

It's already being used—this is exactly what Reuben, a cryptocurrency and blockchain consultant, did to charge his client for 30 minutes consultation. And that's it for Sablier - if you're keen to get started or test it out, we've included a step-by-step guide on how to start streaming payment with Sablier. Otherwise, head on to the next section to read more on the next DeFi app.

## Sablier Step-by-Step Guide:

### Step 1

- Go to pay.sablier.finance
- Sign in with your Ethereum wallet

Step 2
- Select a token from the list
- Type an amount (which will be refunded when the stream finishes earlier)
- Type an ENS domain or Ethereum address
- Select a duration, e.g. 30 day

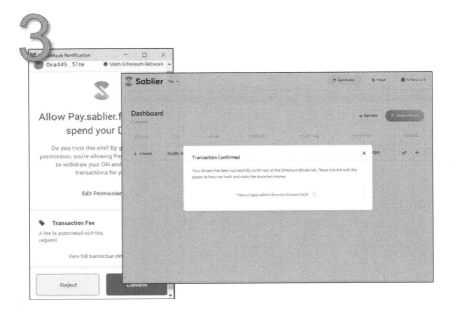

Step 3
- Confirm your transaction

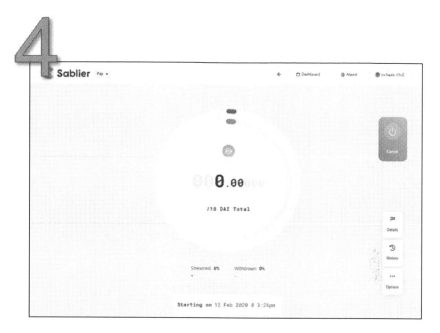

Step 4

- After the blockchain validates your transaction, you will be shown a payment link
- Share this with the owner of the ENS domain/Ethereum address from before

## Recommended Readings

1. Sablier v1 is Live (Paul Razvan Berg)
   https://medium.com/sablier/sablier-v1-is-live-5a5350db16ae
2. Sablier The protocol for real-time finance (State of the Dapps)
   https://www.stateoftheDapps.com/Dapps/sablier
3. Building with Sablier (Sablier)
   https://twitter.com/SablierHQ/status/1214239545220386819?s=19
4. DeFi Dive: Sablier – the protocol for real-time finance on Ethereum
   https://defipulse.com/blog/defi-dive-sablier-protocol/

# CHAPTER 12: DECENTRALIZED INSURANCE

To participate in DeFi, one has to lock tokens in smart contracts. Tokens locked in smart contracts are potentially vulnerable to smart contract exploits due to the large potential payout. While most projects have gotten their codebases audited, one will never know if the smart contracts are truly safe and there is always a possibility of a hack which may result in a loss.

There have been two high-profile DeFi exploits that took place recently involving a DeFi Dapp called bZx. Both exploits happened on the 15th and 18th February 2020 amounting to a total loss of 3,649 ETH or roughly $1 million. The first exploit resulted in a loss of 1,271 ETH and the second exploit resulted in a loss of 2,378 ETH. Both exploits are highly complex transactions that involve multiple DeFi Dapps.

The potential for such massive losses highlights the risks inherent in DeFi and it is something which many people are not paying close attention to. Here are some of the risks that are faced by DeFi users:
1. Technical Risks: where smart contracts could be hacked or bugs could be exploited;
2. Liquidity Risks: where protocols like Compound could run out of liquidity;
3. Admin Key Risks: where the master private key for the protocol could be compromised.

The risks highlight the need for purchasing insurance if one is dealing with large amounts on DeFi. In this section, we will be covering 2 major providers of decentralized insurance to help you protect your DeFi transactions, namely Nexus Mutual and Opyn.

## Nexus Mutual

### What is Nexus Mutual?

Nexus Mutual is a decentralized insurance protocol built on Ethereum that currently offers cover on any smart contract on the Ethereum blockchain. Here's a list of some of the DeFi smart contracts that can be covered by Nexus Mutual:

| Nexus Mutual Supported DeFi Smart Contracts (Feb 2020) | | | |
|---|---|---|---|
| No. | DeFi Smart Contract | No. | DeFi Smart Contract |
| 1 | MakerDAO | 10 | Set Protocol |
| 2 | Moloch DAO | 11 | Fulcrum |
| 3 | Nuo | 12 | Aave |
| 4 | Gnosis | 13 | Compound |
| 5 | 0x | 14 | Edgeware |
| 6 | Tornado Cash | 15 | IDEX |
| 7 | Uniswap | 16 | Instadapp |
| 8 | Argent | 17 | DDEX |
| 9 | dYdX | 18 | Pool Together |

### What event is covered by Nexus Mutual?

Currently, Nexus Mutual offers coverage against smart contract failures, which protects against potential bugs in smart contract code. The coverage may result in protection against financial losses that may be incurred due to hacks or exploits in the smart contract code. Note that smart contract cover only protects against "unintended uses" of smart contracts, so security events such as the loss of private keys or centralized exchange hacks are not covered.

## How does coverage work?

To get started you will first need to choose the Cover Period and the Cover Amount. The Cover Amount is the amount that you would like to purchase cover for and will be the amount that will be paid out in case there are smart contract failures. Upon a smart contract failure incident, a Claims Assessment process will take place that will be evaluated by Claims Assessors. Once it has been approved, the Cover Amount will be paid to you.

## How is the coverage priced?

While all smart contracts can be covered by Nexus Mutual, the price of Smart Contract Cover is based on several criteria such as:

1. The characteristics of the smart contract that requires coverage. Examples include value held in contract, transactions processed etc.
2. Cover Amount
3. Cover Period
4. Value staked by Risk Assessors against the smart contract

A smart contract that does not have sufficient value staked against it or has not been battle-tested enough will return a quote which is un-coverable, meaning that the smart contract cannot be covered at the time.

For example, let's say you buy 5 ETH worth of cover for the Compound smart contract when ETH is $200. Assuming the coverage is 0.013 ETH per 1 ETH of coverage for a year, this would cost you a total of 0.065ETH for a year of coverage. If Compound gets hacked during this period of time, you will be able to get back 5 ETH regardless of the price of ETH during the time of hack. If ETH has risen to $300 during the hack, you would still receive back 5 ETH as long as your claim is approved.

Note that anyone can buy cover on any smart contract and submit a claim once there is an unintended use of the smart contract. You do not need proof that you had funds invested in the smart contract and suffered a loss.

### How to Purchase Cover?

1. Specify which smart contract address you want Cover for.
2. Specify the Cover Amount, currency (ETH or DAI) and Cover Period.
3. Generate a quote and make the transaction using Metamask.
4. You are now covered!

### NXM Token

Nexus Mutual has its own native token known as NXM. The NXM token is used to buy cover, participate in Risk Assessment and Claims Assessment. It is also used to encourage capital provision and represents ownership to the mutual's capital. As the mutual's capital pool increases, the value of NXM will increase as well.

Through the platform, users can do two things - purchase cover for their capital or become a Risk Assessor by staking NXM.

It uses a token bonding curve which is affected by both the amount of capital the mutual has and the amount of capital it needs to meet all claims with a certain probability.

Currently the NXM token is not traded on any exchange and is only used as an internal token for Nexus Mutual.

### What is a Risk Assessor?

A Risk Assessor is someone who stakes value against smart contracts (essentially vouching that the smart contract is safe) and is incentivized to do so by earning rewards in NXM, as users take cover on their staked smart contracts. A Risk Assessor would be someone who understands the risks in solidity smart contracts and either:

(1) assesses individual Dapps themselves, or
(2) trusts someone who says the contract is secure (like an auditor or other staker)

### Has NXM ever paid out claims before?

Yes! In the case of the recent bZx flash loan event, there were 6 members who had cover on the smart contract for a total cover of roughly $87,000.

As of the time of writing, three claims have been accepted so far, receiving their payouts immediately after the Risk Assessors voted to approve their claims.

## Nexus Mutual: Step-by-Step Guide

Step 1
- Go to https://nexusmutual.io/ and click get a quote

Step 2
- Choose Contract that you would like to cover or enter a custom address. We chose the Maker MultiCollateral Dai Contract
- Fill in cover amount and time (cover amount must be in whole numbers)

Step 3
- It will take a while to get a quote

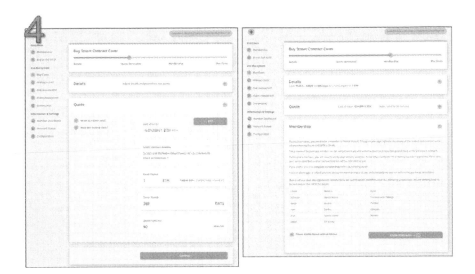

Step 4

- After the quote has been generated, Nexus Mutual will show the cost of cover. Currently, the cost of insurance (payable in ETH) is around 1.3% of the cover. If you are agreeable to this, you may continue and will need to sign up to be a member

## Step 5

- To become a member, you will need to:
  1. Not be a resident in the following countries: China, Japan, Sri Lanka, Ethiopia, Mexico, Syria, North Korea, Trinidad and Tobago, India, Russia, Tunisia, Iran, Serbia, Vanuatu, Iraq, South Korea, Yemen
  2. Complete KYC
  3. Pay one-off membership fee of 0.002ETH
- Once you are done with the KYC, you can proceed with the next steps to buy your insurance.

## Disclaimer

*Due to the restrictions placed on residents of certain countries and the KYC process required to use Nexus Mutual, some people may argue that it is not truly decentralized.*

This is where another insurance product can come into play, Opyn.

**Recommended Readings**

1. A guide to financial risk in DeFi (Seth Goldfarb)
   https://defiprime.com/risks-in-defi
2. The Defiant tweets on the exploits (Camila Russo)
   https://twitter.com/CamiRusso/status/1229849049471373312
3. bZx Hack Analysis Exposes Challenging DeFi-Inherent Composable Liquidity Risks (PeckShield)
   https://blog.peckshield.com/2020/02/15/bZx/
4. bZx Hack Full Disclosure (With Detailed Profit Analysis) (PeckShield) https://blog.peckshield.com/2020/02/17/bZx/
5. bZx Hack II Full Disclosure (With Detailed Profit Analysis) (PeckShield) https://blog.peckshield.com/2020/02/18/bZx/
6. Nexus Mutual NXM Token Explainer (Hugh Karp)
   https://medium.com/nexus-mutual/nexus-mutual-nxm-token-explainer-b468bc537543
7. Nexus Mutual (Fitzner Blockchain)
   https://tokentuesdays.substack.com/p/nexus-mutual
8. The Potential for Bonding Curves and Nexus Mutual (Fitzner Blockchain) https://tokentuesdays.substack.com/p/the-potential-for-bonding-curves
9. Why Nexus Mutual should be on your radar (Defi Dad)
   https://twitter.com/DeFi_Dad/status/1227165545608335360?s=09

# Opyn

## What is Opyn?

Opyn is another DeFi app that provides insurance for smart contracts. Currently, Opyn has protection for USDC and DAI deposits on Compound and stablecoin deposits on another DeFi dapp, Curve.

Opyn provides protection against a number of risks beyond smart contract failures such as financial risks and admin risks. Opyn does this by making use of financial derivatives, namely options.

## What are Options?

There are two kinds of options, Call option and Put option. A Call option is a right, but not the obligation to purchase an asset at a specific strike price within a specific period of time. A Put option on the other hand is a right, but not the obligation to sell an asset at a specific strike price within a specific period of time.

For every purchaser of an option, there must be a seller of an option. A purchaser of an option will pay a premium to the seller of the option to get this right.

Here is a Halloween analogy of a Call option to better help your understanding of options:

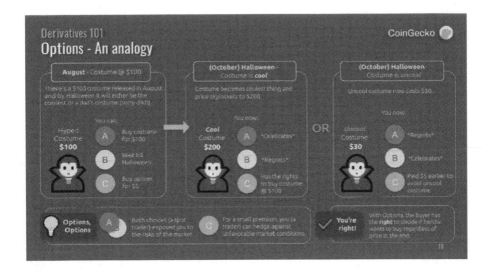

There are two main options flavors, namely American and European options. The difference between the two is that for an American option, the buyer can exercise the option anytime before the expiry date whereas for an European option, the buyer can only exercise it only on the strike date.

## How does Opyn work?

Opyn allows users to hedge against the risk of a black swan event happening on Compound by allowing users to buy Put options on USDC and DAI stablecoin deposits.

As mentioned earlier in the Compound section, when someone loans DAI, they would get cDAI tokens in return. By using Opyn, a trader can buy oTokens which can be used as a right to sell cDAI and get back DAI in case there is a smart contract failure on Compound.

Purchasing 1 DAI worth of insurance on Opyn is essentially buying an American Put option for the cDAI asset with a strike price of $0.92. In the event that Compound fails, any DAI deposits on Compound will no longer be worth $1.00 but significantly less, say for example $0.10. With Opyn's ocDAI token, the insurance purchaser is able to redeem $0.92 back, payable in ETH. This protects the user against smart contract losses. No centralized entity is needed to verify the claim making this a truly decentralized insurance.

**Important note: Opyn covers only your principal deposit and not any interest that you may have accrued on Compound. When you deposit your DAI on Compound you get cDAI in return. To make a claim on Opyn, you send your cDAI and oDAI insurance tokens to Opyn and immediately receive your coverage amount.**

## How much does Insurance cost?

As of the time of writing, buying insurance on Compound using Opyn costs roughly the following Annual Percentage Rate: 1.22% on Dai deposits and 2.61% on USDC deposits. This means that if you are earning 5.41% uninsured yield on Dai deposits, after purchasing insurance on Opyn, you are guaranteed a 4.19% yield.

Do note that Opyn is still relatively new, having just launched in February 2020 and the cost of insurance may fluctuate as the market finds an optimal equilibrium.

Because the insurance is tokenized in the form of oTokens, they can be traded on DEXs like Uniswap which is why the price of the insurance would be dependent on the market price that is determined based on the supply and demand.

## Why would anyone provide insurance on Opyn?

For every purchaser of insurance (purchaser of Put option) on Opyn, there must be a provider of insurance (seller of Put option) on Opyn. By being an insurance provider on Opyn, an ETH holder can earn a yield on their ETH.

To do so, one starts by supplying ETH as collateral to Opyn's smart contract at a minimum collateralization ratio of 160% to mint oTokens. Insurance providers can mint oTokens for either USDC or DAI on Compound.

Once oTokens have been minted, there are two exciting ways to earn premium:

1. Being a Liquidity Provider on Uniswap

   As a Liquidity Provider on Uniswap, one can earn transaction fees from individuals buying and selling on the Opyn platform through Uniswap. Liquidity Providers have the opportunity to make a large but variable return from providing liquidity on Uniswap. Liquidity Providers are allowed to remove funds at any time. Our section on Uniswap shows you the steps to provide liquidity on Uniswap.

2. Selling oTokens on Uniswap

   The oTokens that have been minted can be sold on Uniswap. To calculate the Annual Percentage Rate for selling oTokens on Uniswap, you can look at Opyn's main dashboard and calculate the difference between the uninsured yield and insured yield since this is what a user would give up to get insured. As of the time of writing, the Annual Percentage Rate that can be obtained is 1.22% on DAI and 2.61% on USDC.

The premiums that can be earned on the ETH collateral is higher than anywhere else in DeFi. However, earning this yield does not come without risk. By selling the Put option for a yield, the option seller assumes the risk that there will not be a disaster event (e.g. technical risk like a hack, financial risk like DAI breaking its peg or a run on Compound). One must also maintain a collateral ratio above 160% so as not to be liquidated.

## Is Opyn safe?

Opyn has a publicly verifiable smart contract and its smart contract has been audited by OpenZeppelin, a smart contract auditing firm. The full report is available here: https://blog.openzeppelin.com/opyn-contracts-audit/.

Opyn is also noncustodial and trustless, with a reliance on incentives for it to work.

## What are the key differences between Nexus Mutual and Opyn?

|  | Nexus Mutual | Opyn |
|---|---|---|
| **Covers Against** | Smart Contract Hacks | Technical, financial, admin key risks |
| **Claims Approval** | Yes – Voting | No – immediate withdrawal upon claim |
| **Liquidity** | Coverage Pools | Two-Sided Market |
| **Fully Collateralized** | No | Yes |
| **Common Capital Pool** | Yes | No |
| **Pricing** | Nexus pricing algorithm & Risk Assessors | Depends on the supply and demand of the market, mainly via Uniswap |

## Opyn: Step-by-Step Guide

### Step 1

- Go to https://opyn.co/ and click get started. We will be insuring some DAI on Compound

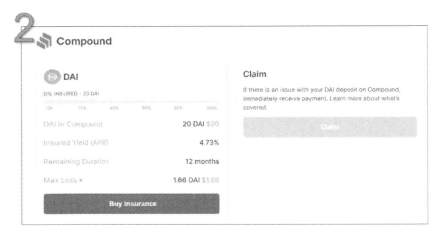

### Step 2

- Since we have 20 DAI on Compound, we wish to buy insurance for them

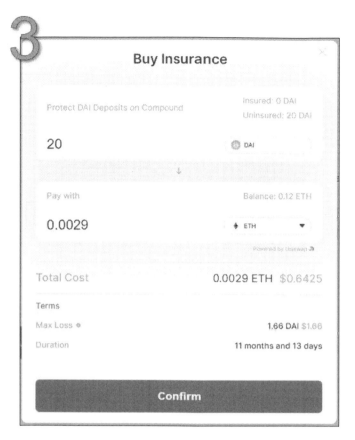

Step 3
- After clicking Buy Insurance, we will be redirected here
- Click confirm and confirm the transaction

Step 4
- As you can see we got ocDai in exchange for our ETH
- Note that the amounts are different. 1 ocDAI covers 1 cDAI, not 1 DAI. Remember, in the earlier chapter that 1 DAI does not get you 1 cDAI

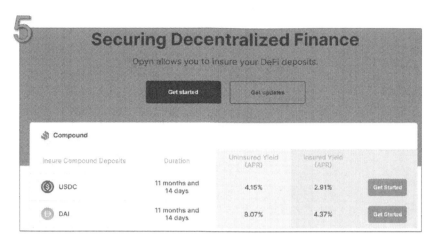

**Step 5**

- After the transaction is confirmed, if you wish to check whether you compound DAI is insured, just proceed back to Opyn's get started page for Dai

**Step 6**

- You'll see your insured amount there

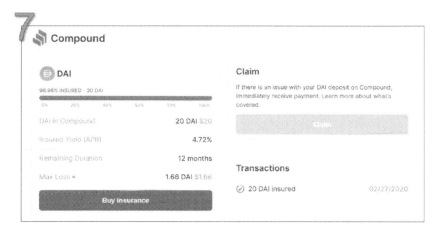

Step 7
- And when you go into the Dai page you'll see under transactions that there is 20 DAI insured.

## Conclusion

One thing to note is that because the pricing of oTokens is determined by demand and supply, one can use this as a signaling mechanism to check if there is something wrong with Compound. If people believe that a black swan event is going to happen on Compound, they would start purchasing more oTokens and the oTokens would increase in price.

At the end of the day, the choice to insure or not to insure is ultimately up to you, the user. However, we at CoinGecko definitely recommend purchasing insurance as we never know what could happen especially in the still nascent DeFi markets.

## Recommended Readings

1. Convexity Protocol Announcement (Zubin Koticha) https://twitter.com/snarkyzk/status/1194442219530280960
2. Options Protocol Brings 'Insurance' to DeFi Deposits on Compound (Brady Dale) https://www.coindesk.com/options-protocol-brings-insurance-to-defi-deposits-on-compound
3. Getting Started (Opyn) https://opyn.gitbook.io/opyn/
4. Opyn launches insurance platform to protect DeFi users (Zubin Koticha) https://medium.com/opyn/opyn-launches-insurance-platform-to-protect-defi-users-fdcabaca7d97
5. Exploring the Decentralized Insurance Arena That's Rising on Ethereum (William Peaster) https://blockonomi.com/decentralized-insurance-ethereum/

# CHAPTER 13: DEFI DASHBOARD

## What is a Dashboard?

A dashboard is a simple platform that aggregates all your DeFi activities in one place. It is a useful tool to visualize and track where your assets are across the different DeFi protocols. The dashboard is able to segregate your assets into different categories such as deposit, debt and investments.

Typically when you access your dashboard, you will need to enter your Ethereum address (e.g.: *0x4Cdc86fa95Ec2704f0849825f1F8b077deeD8d39*). Alternatively, you could enter your Ethereum Name Service (ENS) domain. ENS domain is a human-readable Ethereum address that you can purchase for a period of time. It is similar to Internet domain names such as www.coingecko.com which then maps to the IP address of the server where CoinGecko is hosted.

Check out our ENS guide at https://www.coingecko.com/buzz/coingecko-guide-to-ethereum-name-service-ens if you are interested in creating your own ENS domain!
*Note: ENS domain is completely optional.*

There are several dashboards in the market with the capacity to track your assets like Frontier, InstaDApp, MyDeFi and Zerion. For simplicity, we will look into one of the more known dashboards called DeFiSnap.

## DeFiSnap: Step-by-Step Guide

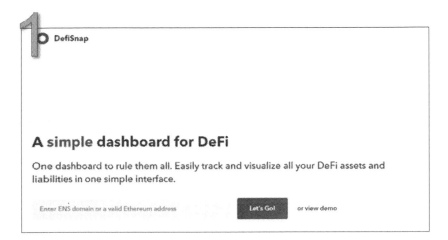

Step 1
- Go to https://www.defisnap.io
- Enter your ENS domain or your Ethereum Address
- Here I used defiportal.eth but I can also key in 0x358a6c0f7614c44b344381b0699e2397b1483252

Step 2
- You are on the dashboard!
- You can see your wallet balance, and any DeFi deposits, debt and investments.

Alternatively, you can check out other dashboards:
- https://mydefi.org/apps
- https://unspent.io/
- https://zerion.io/
- https://frontierwallet.com/ (Dashboard for mobile phones)

# PART FOUR: DEFI IN ACTION

# CHAPTER 14: DEFI IN ACTION

In the previous sections, we talked about the importance of DeFi and showed some of the products available in the DeFi ecosystem. However, questions still remain on how decentralized DeFi Dapps are and if there is anyone actually using DeFi in real life. In this section, we will explore DeFi in action with two case studies showing the robustness and usefulness of DeFi.

## Surviving Argentina's High Inflation

During the Devcon 5 Ethereum conference in October 2019, Mariano Conti, Head of Smart Contracts at Maker Foundation gave a talk on how he survives Argentina's inflation. The inflation rate for Argentina reached 53.8% in 2019, the highest rate in 28 years. This placed Argentina as the top 5 countries in the world with the highest inflation rates.[17]

---

[17] "Argentina inflation expected at 53% in December ... – Reuters." 11 Sep. 2019, https://www.reuters.com/article/argentina-economy/argentina-inflation-expected-at-53-in-december-2019-treasury-officials-idINKCN1VX09U.

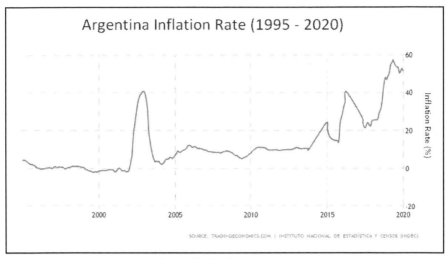

*Source: TradingEconomics.com*

To live in a country where the value of your national currency practically halves every year is tough. To survive in Argentina, Mariano requested for his salary to be fully paid in DAI. As you may know from our previous section, DAI is a stablecoin pegged to the USD. According to Mariano, Argentinians value the USD a lot. Despite the USD having problems like it being inflationary as well, compared to the Argentine Peso, it is nothing.

If the USD is attractive to most Argentinians, it is natural then that most Argentinians would prefer to keep their money in USD. However, the government in Argentina places capital control on this, making it hard to get access to the USD. There is a limit on the purchase of USD and Argentinians can only purchase a maximum of $200 per month. As a result of this, the black market demand for the USD has risen, causing the exchange rate to be approximately 30% higher than the officially declared rate by the government.[18]

Besides placing a limit on purchases, the Central Bank of Argentina also exposed 800 citizens' names, ID number and tax identification because they exceeded the previous purchase limit of $10,000.[19] Furthermore,

----

[18] "Argentina's 'little trees' blossom as forex controls fuel black ..." 5 Feb. 2020, https://www.reuters.com/article/us-argentina-currency-blackmarket/argentinas-little-trees-blossom-as-forex-controls-fuel-black-market-idUSKBN1ZZ1H1.

[19] "Argentina Central Bank Exposed 800 Citizens ... – BeInCrypto." 29 Sep. 2019, https://beincrypto.com/argentina-central-bank-exposed-sensitive-information-

Argentinians who work for foreign companies and are invoiced in USD must liquidate their USD to Argentine Peso within 5 days.

According to Mariano, several years ago, many Argentinian freelancers preferred getting paid in Bitcoin. While this worked well in the earlier years prior to 2018 when Bitcoin price was on an uptrend, as the market turned downwards, there was an urgent need to convert Bitcoin immediately to Argentine Peso otherwise their salary will be greatly reduced. While Bitcoin provided many Argentinians with an alternative way of being paid, the volatile nature of Bitcoin meant that there was a need for "better money".

For Mariano, DAI is the solution to this problem as it has all the advantages of cryptocurrencies while staying pegged to the USD. But what does he do with his DAI? Once a month, he withdraws the bare minimum to pay for items like rent, groceries and credit card bill, keeping his Argentine Peso balance as close to 0 as possible.

He also uses his DAI for crypto transactions, such as purchasing ETH and putting DAI into Dai Savings Rate. From this, he is able to earn interest on a stablecoin which he would otherwise not have access to. While he does acknowledge that by using DeFi Dapps, he exposes himself to risks such as smart contract or platform risks, he feels that the risk of holding Argentinian Peso is high as well.

To Mariano, being paid in DAI allows him to "escape" issues such as volatility, inflation, and control facing his country. This issue is not just facing Argentina but by several other economies in the world, and this is proof of how DeFi can be valuable for people living in these countries.

To watch his full presentation, do click this link here:
https://slideslive.com/38920018/living-on-defi-how-i-survive-argentinas-50-inflation.

## Uniswap Ban

---

of-800-citizens/.

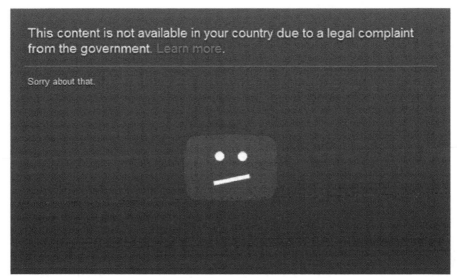

*Looks familiar? (Image Credit: gtricks.com[20])*

Most of us have likely seen this—a video or mobile app which has been made unavailable to us because of our location or due to censorships. It's infuriating, it's annoying, but life goes on—you can find the video elsewhere or simply download another similar application for the same service.

Bans on videos, apps or may not have overly adverse effects, but the same cannot be said if it was the access to bank or financial institution that was banned. This unfortunately hits hardest on those who need it most, as they likely do not keep large amounts of extra cash on hand. A person may be forced to take loans to cover their expenses, potentially snowballing to many other things down the road.

That being said, within the DeFi ecosystem censorships have happened as well. One notable occasion was the Uniswap (decentralized exchange) geographical ban back in December 2019. At that time, the Uniswap team quietly updated and published a change to their open-sourced codebase on Github[21] to exclude certain countries (Belarus, Cuba, Iran, Iraq, Côte

---

[20] "Watch YouTube Blocked Videos Not Available in Your Country." https://www.gtricks.com/youtube/watch-blocked-youtube-videos-not-available-in-your-country/. Accessed 27 Feb. 2020.

d'Ivoire, Liberia, North Korea, Sudan, Syria, Zimbabwe) from accessing the main website at www.uniswap.exchange. The result looks like this:

*With the geoblock in place, people from the blocked countries can no longer access the Uniswap.exchange website.*

Word on the street is that the Uniswap team had to do so to remain compliant with US laws as their team is based in New York. Regardless of the reason, if Uniswap were to make their services inaccessible to people because of their location, it would go against everything DeFi stands for - which is to allow **anyone** to have access from **anywhere.**

In upholding the true spirits of DeFi, the geographical ban Uniswap team imposed did not stop users from using the Uniswap protocol - in fact, they couldn't. The Uniswap protocol is built and deployed on the Ethereum blockchain (which is accessible worldwide by anyone). Within a matter of hours, multiple sites that are connected to the Uniswap protocol have gone live, enabling users who were previously banned to continue accessing the Uniswap protocol.

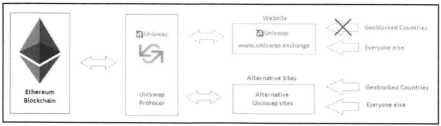

*Since Uniswap protocol is permissionless, anyone can connect to it if they know how to, or have an interface (like uniswap.exchange website) that allows them to.*

---

21 "Uniswap/uniswap-frontend: □ An open-source ... – GitHub." https://github.com/Uniswap/uniswap-frontend. Accessed 27 Feb. 2020.

The key point to note in this incident is that, while the Uniswap team had control of the frontend (www.uniswap.exchange), they had no control over who can or cannot access the backend (Uniswap protocol) deployed onto the Ethereum blockchain.

This was a very interesting case study as it highlighted the strengths of DeFi protocols, something that would not happen in traditional finance. **A move that was initially made to go against the very core ethos of DeFi ended up showcasing one of its key strengths**.

This is not the first, and will not be the last time DeFi applications are challenged. It will be exciting to see what the future holds!

# CHAPTER 15: DEFI IS THE FUTURE, AND THE FUTURE IS NOW

DeFi represents the future of finance. While this can sound controversial, we are going to summarize here why we think that is the case.

At the start of 2020, the Total Value Locked in DeFi Dapps hit the significant milestone of $1 billion. In other words, that's the total amount of programmable money currently stored in smart contracts that serve as the building blocks of an entirely new decentralized financial system on the internet.

While $1 billion locked into DeFi may seem like a small number compared to traditional financial markets, the growth has been staggering. Here's a quick summary of the journey:
- 2018: Total Value Locked increased 5 times from $50 million to $275 million
- 2019: Total Value Locked increased 2.4 times to $667 million
- 2020: Total Value Locked reached $1 billion (Feb 2020)

Before we push on, let's have a quick recap on some of the things DeFi allows us to achieve:

**Transparency:** A transparent, auditable financial ecosystem.

**Accessibility:** Free access to DeFi applications without fear of discrimination on race, gender, beliefs, nationality or geographical status.

**Efficiency:** Programmable money makes it possible to remove the centralized middlemen to create a more affordable and efficient financial market.

**Convenience:** Money can now be sent anywhere, anytime and to anyone who has access to a cryptocurrency wallet for a small fee and with little waiting time.

All of the above have made it possible for users to do some of the following: provide liquidity to earn yields on unproductive assets with no maturation/lock-in period, take loans (with collateral) without paperwork and repay them anytime, and execute automated trading strategies easily.

Perhaps the best thing is that all of the above can be accessed by anyone, anywhere, anytime as long as they are connected to the Internet. Now that's the power of DeFi in terms of accessibility and we're only just getting started on this journey.

## What about DeFi User Experience?

We're glad you asked - while accessibility to DeFi apps may be a non-issue, one of the major pain points for DeFi remains the overall user experience.

That said, many teams worldwide are hard at work trying to improve the experience. Have a look at some of them and the aspects they are attempting to solve:

**Wallet:** Argent (https://www.argent.xyz/) is creating a radically better user-focused crypto wallet experience, with free transactions on Ethereum without needing ETH, native integration with Compound (and others), as well as not needing seed keys.

**Participation of products:** DeFiZap (https://defizap.com/) abstracts away many of the complexities and steps involved with DeFi products and allows users to access multiple financial products in one transaction, saving time and effort.

**User-friendly development:** Gelato Finance (https://play.gelato.finance/) recently launched their "If this, then that" for crypto. It basically allows users to set actions that will be done once certain conditions are met, such as "Buy ETH when it is $200", or "Send some money to Alice when it's her birthday".

**Insurance:** Financial market effectively facilitates the transfer of risk. One man's hedge against his position is another man's profit. Insurance is now available as we've covered earlier via Nexus Mutual or Opyn. If you are willing to accept a lower yield on the money you've placed on lending protocols such as Compound in exchange for peace of mind, it can now be done.

**Aggregation of liquidity:** There are many different decentralized exchanges (DEXes) in the market with varying liquidity and it is a headache for users to choose which one is the best for their trade. This is slowly becoming a thing of the past with liquidity aggregators such as 1inch.exchange, Paraswap and DEX.AG that helps to automatically split orders across DEXes to ensure best possible prices.

**Yield optimization:** Remember switching around different banks for the best rates for fixed deposits? You don't have to do that in DeFi—yield bouncers like idle.finance, DeFiSaver and iEarn automatically allocate your cryptoassets to places with the best yield opportunities on the Ethereum blockchain.

While there is no single "killer app" that bridges the user experience gap at the moment, we think it's not going to be far away!

# CLOSING REMARKS

Phew, that was a blast to write! If you are reading this line here, congratulations, you are now up to date on DeFi and you should give yourself a pat on the back!

Thank you for your time and we hope you've enjoyed this read as much as we've enjoyed researching, learning and writing it! :)

Welcome to DeFi and the future of finance!

# APPENDIX

## CoinGecko's Recommended DeFi Resources

### Information
DeFi Prime - https://defiprime.com/
DeFi Pulse - https://defipulse.com/
DeFi Tutorials - https://defitutorials.com/
LoanScan - http://loanscan.io/

### Newsletters
Bankless - https://bankless.substack.com/
DeFi Tutorials - https://defitutorials.substack.com/
DeFi Weekly - https://defiweekly.substack.com/
Dose of DeFi - https://doseofdefi.substack.com/
Ethhub - https://ethhub.substack.com/
My Two Gwei - https://mytwogwei.substack.com/
The Defiant - https://thedefiant.substack.com/
Week in Ethereum News - https://www.weekinethereumnews.com/

### Podcast
BlockCrunch - https://castbox.fm/channel/Blockcrunch%3A-Crypto-Deep-Dives-id1182347
Chain Reaction - https://fiftyonepercent.podbean.com/
Into the Ether - Ethhub - https://podcast.ethhub.io/
PoV Crypto - https://povcryptopod.libsyn.com/

Wyre Podcast - https://blog.sendwyre.com/wyretalks/home

## Youtube
Chris Blec - https://www.youtube.com/c/chrisblec

## Bankless Level-Up Guide
https://bankless.substack.com/p/bankless-level-up-guide

## Projects We Like Too
### Dashboard Interfaces
DeFi Prime Portfolio - http://portfolio.defiprime.com
Frontier - https://frontierwallet.com/
InstaDApp - https://instadapp.io/
MyDeFi - https://mydefi.org/apps
Zerion - https://zerion.io/

### Decentralized Exchanges
Bancor - https://www.bancor.network/
Curve Finance - https://www.curve.fi/
Dex Blue https://dex.blue/
Kyber - https://kyberswap.com/swap

### Exchange Aggregators
1inch - https://1inch.exchange/
Dex.ag - https://dex.ag/
Paraswap - https://paraswap.io/

### Lending and Borrowing
Dharma - https://www.dharma.io/

### Prediction Markets
Augur - https://www.augur.net/

### Taxes
TokenTax - https://tokentax.co/

Wallet
**GnosisSafe** - https://safe.gnosis.io/
**Monolith** - https://monolith.xyz/

Yield Optimisers
**Iearn** - https://iearn.finance/
**RAY** https://staked.us/v/robo-advisor-yield/

# References

## Chapter 1: Traditional Financial Institutions

Bagnall, E. (2019, June 30). Top 1000 World Banks 2019 – The Banker International Press Release – for immediate release. Retrieved February 20, 2020, from https://www.thebanker.com/Top-1000-World-Banks/Top-1000-World-Banks-2019-The-Banker-International-Press-Release-for-immediate-release

Boehlke, J. (2019, September 18). How Long Does It Take to Have a Payment Post Online to Your Bank? Retrieved February 20, 2020, from https://www.gobankingrates.com/banking/checking-account/how-long-payment-posted-online-account/

Demirguc-Kunt, A., Klapper, L., Singer, D., Ansar, S., Hess, J. (2018).The Global Findex Database 2017: Measuring Financial Inclusion and the Fintech Revolution. https://doi.org/10.1596/978-1-4648-1259-0_ch2

How long does an Ethereum transaction really take? (2019, September 25). Retrieved February 20, 2020, from https://ethgasstation.info/blog/ethereum-transaction-how-long/

International Wire Transfers. (n.d.). Retrieved February 20, 2020, from https://www.bankofamerica.com/foreign-exchange/wire-transfer.go

Karlan, D., Ratan, A. L., & Zinman, J. (2014, March). Savings by and for the poor: a research review and agenda. Retrieved February 20, 2020, from https://www.ncbi.nlm.nih.gov/pmc/articles/PMC4358152/

Stably. (2019, September 20). Decentralized Finance vs. Traditional Finance: What You Need To Know. Retrieved from https://medium.com/stably-blog/decentralized-finance-vs-traditional-finance-what-you-need-to-know-3b57aed7a0c2

## Chapter 2: What is Decentralized Finance (DeFi)?

Campbell, L. (2020, January 6). DeFi Market Report for 2019 - Summary of DeFi Growth in 2019. Retrieved from https://defirate.com/market-report-2019/

Mitra, R. (n.d.). DeFi Use cases: The Best Examples of Decentralised Finance. Retrieved from https://blockgeeks.com/guides/defi-use-cases-the-best-examples-of-decentralised-finance/#_Tool_2_DeFi_Derivatives

Shawdagor, J. (2020, February 23). Sectors Realizing the Full Potential of DeFi Protocols In 2020. Retrieved from https://cointelegraph.com/news/sectors-realizing-the-full-potential-of-defi-protocols-in-2020

Thompson, P. (2020, January 5). Most Significant Hacks of 2019 - New Record of Twelve in One Year. Retrieved February 20, 2020, from https://cointelegraph.com/news/most-significant-hacks-of-2019-new-record-of-twelve-in-one-year

## Chapter 3: The Decentralized Layer: Ethereum

What is Ethereum? (2020, February 11). Retrieved from https://ethereum.org/what-is-ethereum/

Rosic, A. (2018). What is Ethereum Gas? [The Most Comprehensive Step-By-Step Guide!]. Retrieved from https://blockgeeks.com/guides/ethereum-gas/

Rosic, A. (2017). What Are Smart Contracts? [Ultimate Beginner's Guide to Smart Contracts]. Retrieved from https://blockgeeks.com/guides/smart-contracts/

## Chapter 4: Ethereum Wallets

Lee, I. (2018, June 22). A Complete Beginner's Guide to Using MetaMask. Retrieved from https://www.coingecko.com/buzz/complete-beginners-guide-to-metamask

Lesuisse, I. (2018, December 22). A new era for crypto security. Retrieved from https://medium.com/argenthq/a-new-era-for-crypto-security-57909a095ae3

Wright, M. (2020, February 13). Argent: The quick start guide. Retrieved from https://medium.com/argenthq/argent-the-quick-start-guide-13541ce2b1fb

## Chapter 5: Decentralized Stablecoins

The Maker Protocol: MakerDAO's Multi-Collateral Dai (MCD) System (n.d.). Retrieved February 20, 2020, from https://makerdao.com/whitepaper/

MKR Tools (n.d.). Retrieved February 20, 2020, from https://mkr.tools/governance/stabilityfee

Maker Governance Dashboard (n.d.). Retrieved February 20, 2020, from https://vote.makerdao.com/pollin

Currency Re-imagined for the World: Multi-Collateral Dai Is Live! (2019, November 18). Retrieved from https://blog.makerdao.com/multi-collateral-dai-is-live/

Dai is now live! (2017, December 19). Retrieved from https://blog.makerdao.com/dai-is-now-live/

DSR. (n.d.). Retrieved February 20, 2020, from https://community-development.makerdao.com/makerdao-mcd-faqs/faqs/dsr

John, J. (2019, December 4). Stable Coins In 2019. Retrieved from https://www.decentralised.co/what-is-going-on-with-stable-coins/

Tether: Fiat currencies on the Bitcoin blockchain. (n.d.). Tether Whitepaper. Retrieved from https://tether.to/wp-content/uploads/2016/06/TetherWhitePaper.pdf

## Chapter 6: Decentralized Borrowing and Lending

Leshner, R. (2018, December 6). Compound FAQ. Retrieved from
  https://medium.com/compound-finance/faq-1a2636713b69

## Chapter 7: Decentralized Exchange (DEX)

Connect to Uniswap. (n.d.). Retrieved from
  https://docs.uniswap.io/frontend-integration/connect-to-
  uniswap#factory-contract

Juliano, A. (2017). dYdX: A Standard for Decentralized Margin Trading and
  Derivatives. Retrieved from https://whitepaper.dydx.exchange/

Uniswap: Stats, Charts and Guide: DeFi Pulse. (n.d.). Retrieved from
  https://defipulse.com/uniswap

Uniswap Whitepaper. (n.d.). Retrieved from
  https://hackmd.io/@Uniswap/HJ9jLsfTz

Yin, Z. (2020, February). What happens at expiration? Retrieved from
  https://help.dydx.exchange/en/articles/2906752-what-happens-at-
  expiration

Yin, Z. (2020, February). What is liquidation and when will liquidation
  occur? Retrieved from https://help.dydx.exchange/en/articles/2906496-
  what-is-liquidation-and-when-will-liquidation-occur

Zhang, Y., Chen, X., & Park, D. (2018). Formal Specification of Constant
  Product (x x y = k) Market Maker Model and Implementation. Retrieved
  from https://github.com/runtimeverification/verified-smart-
  contracts/blob/uniswap/uniswap/x-y-k.pdf

## Chapter 8: Decentralized Derivatives

Tulip Mania (n.d.). Retrieved from
  https://penelope.uchicago.edu/~grout/encyclopaedia_romana/aconite/t
  ulipomania.html

Chen, J. (2020, January 27). Derivative. Retrieved from
https://www.investopedia.com/terms/d/derivative.asp

Decentralised synthetic assets. (n.d.). Retrieved from
https://www.synthetix.io/products/exchange/
Synthetix.Exchange Overview. (2019, February 15). Retrieved from
https://blog.synthetix.io/synthetix-exchange-overview/

Synthethix Litepaper v1.3. (2019). Retrieved from
https://www.synthetix.io/uploads/synthetix_litepaper.pdf

## Chapter 9: Decentralized Fund Management

Making Sense of the Mutual Fund Scandal Everything you may not want to
ask (but really should know) about the crisis that's rocking the investment
world. (2003, November 24). Retrieved from
https://money.cnn.com/magazines/fortune/fortune_archive/2003/11/2
4/353794/index.htm

The Editors of Encyclopaedia Britannica. (2020, February 26). Bernie
Madoff. Retrieved from https://www.britannica.com/biography/Bernie-
Madoff

Frequently Asked Questions on TokenSets. (n.d.). Retrieved from
https://www.tokensets.com/faq

Liang, R. (2019, April 23). TokenSets is Live: Automate your Crypto
Portfolio Now. Retrieved from https://medium.com/set-
protocol/tokensets-is-live-automate-your-crypto-portfolio-now-
50f88dcc928d
Sawinyh, N. (2019, June 17). Interview with TokenSets creators. Retrieved
from https://defiprime.com/tokensets

Sassano, A. (2019, June 19). How Set Protocol Works Under the Hood.
Retrieved from https://medium.com/@AnthonySassano/how-set-
protocol-works-under-the-hood-74fcdae858e2

Sassano, A. (2020, January 22). Set Social Trading is Now Live on TokenSets. Retrieved from https://medium.com/set-protocol/set-social-trading-is-now-live-on-tokensets-c981b5e67c5f

## Chapter 10: Decentralized Lottery

Cusack, L. (2020, February 3). PoolTogether raises $1 Million to Expand Prize Linked Savings Protocol. Retrieved from https://medium.com/pooltogether/pooltogether-raises-1-million-to-expand-prize-linked-savings-protocol-eb51a1f88ed8

Guillén, M.F., Tschoegl, A.E. Banking on Gambling: Banks and Lottery-Linked Deposit Accounts. Journal of Financial Services Research 21, 219–231 (2002). https://doi.org/10.1023/A:1015081427038

H.148. (2019). Retrieved from https://legislature.vermont.gov/bill/status/2020/H.148

Lemke, T. (2019, February 21). What Are Prize-Linked Savings Accounts? Retrieved from https://www.thebalance.com/what-are-prize-linked-savings-accounts-4587608

LLC, P. T. (n.d.). PoolTogether. Retrieved from https://www.pooltogether.com/#stats

Markets. (n.d.). Retrieved from https://compound.finance/markets

PoolTogether. (2020, February 8). Wow! The winner of the largest prize ever only 10 Dai deposited! They won $1,648 Dai A 1 in 69,738 chance of winning. Congrats to the little fish! pic.twitter.com/0DSFkSdbIE. Retrieved from https://twitter.com/PoolTogether_/status/1225875154019979265

Texas Proposition 7, Financial Institutions to Offer Prizes to Promote Savings Amendment (2017). (2017). Retrieved from Texas Proposition 7, Financial Institutions to Offer Prizes to Promote Savings Amendment (2017)

## Chapter 11: Decentralized Payment

Bramanathan, R. (2020, February 1). What I learned from tokenizing myself. Retrieved from https://medium.com/@bramanathan/what-i-learned-from-tokenizing-myself-bb222da07906

## Chapter 12: Decentralized Insurance

Blockchain, F. (2019, December 4). The Potential for Bonding Curves and Nexus Mutual. Retrieved from https://tokentuesdays.substack.com/p/the-potential-for-bonding-curves

Blockchain, F. (2019, October 2). Nexus Mutual. Retrieved from https://tokentuesdays.substack.com/p/nexus-mutual

Codefi Data. (n.d.). Retrieved from https://defiscore.io/

defidad.eth, D. F. D.-. (2020, February 11). @NexusMutual is a decentralized alternative to insurance, providing the #Ethereum community protection against hacks. Here's why it should be on your radar:☐Anyone can buy smart contract insurance☐Being a backer (staker) can earn up to 50% ROI☐It's powered by #Ethereum. Retrieved from https://twitter.com/DeFi_Dad/status/1227165545608335360?s=09

Docs. (n.d.). Retrieved from https://nexusmutual.gitbook.io/docs/docs#pricing

Karp, H. (2019, May 22). Nexus Mutual Audit Report. Retrieved from https://medium.com/nexus-mutual/nexus-mutual-audit-report-57f1438d653b

Karp, H. (2019, June 5). Nexus Mutual NXM Token Explainer. Retrieved from https://medium.com/nexus-mutual/nexus-mutual-nxm-token-explainer-b468bc537543

Russo, C. (2020, February 19). Arbs made ~$900K in seconds by exploiting DeFi. It's mind-blowing stuff. Here's The Defiant post w/ exploits' twisted steps (in pics), qs raised about decentralization and price oracles, and consequences so far. What's your take on the blame game? Retrieved from https://twitter.com/CamiRusso/status/1229849049471373312

Token Model. (n.d.). Nexus Mutual: A decentralised alternative to insurance. Retrieved from https://nexusmutual.io/token-model

Welcome to the Nexus Mutual Gitbook. (n.d.). Retrieved from https://nexusmutual.gitbook.io/docs/

Coingecko. (2019). CoinGecko Quarterly Report for Q3 2019. Retrieved from https://assets.coingecko.com/reports/2019-Q3-Report/CoinGecko-2019-Q3-Report.pdf

Defiprime. (2020, February 13). what's the key difference vs. @NexusMutual ? Retrieved from https://twitter.com/defiprime/status/1227720835898560513

Karp, H. (2019, November 15). Comparing Insurance Like Solutions in DeFi. Retrieved from https://medium.com/@hugh_karp/comparing-insurance-like-solutions-in-defi-a804a6be6d48

OpenZeppelin Security. (2020, February 10). Opyn Contracts Audit. Retrieved from https://blog.openzeppelin.com/opyn-contracts-audit/

## Chapter 13: Dashboard

Dashboard for DeFi. (n.d.). Retrieved from https://www.defisnap.io/#/dashboard

## Chapter 14: DeFi in Action

(n.d.). Retrieved October 19, 2019, from https://slideslive.com/38920018/living-on-defi-how-i-survive-argentinas-50-inflation

Gundiuc, C. (2019, September 29). Argentina Central Bank Exposed 800 Citizens' Sensitive Information. Retrieved from https://beincrypto.com/argentina-central-bank-exposed-sensitive-information-of-800-citizens/

Lopez, J. M. S. (2020, February 5). Argentina's 'little trees' blossom as forex controls fuel black market. Retrieved from
https://www.reuters.com/article/us-argentina-currency-blackmarket/argentinas-little-trees-blossom-as-forex-controls-fuel-black-market-idUSKBN1ZZ1H1

Russo, C. (2019, December 9). Uniswap Website Geo-Ban Can't Stop DeFi. Retrieved from https://thedefiant.substack.com/p/uniswap-website-geo-ban-cant-stop-370

# GLOSSARY

| Index | Term | Description |
|---|---|---|
| # | | |
| A | Annual Percentage Yield (APY) | It is an annualized return on saving or investment and the interest is compounded based on the period. |
| | Admin Key Risk | It refers to the risk where the master private key for the protocol could be compromised. |
| | Automated Market Maker (AMM) | Automated Market Maker removes the need for a human to manually quote bid and ask prices in an order book and replaces it with an algorithm. |
| | Audit | Auditing is a systematic process of examining an organization's records to ensure fair and accurate information the organization claims to represent. Smart contract audit refers to the practice of reviewing the smart contract code to find vulnerabilities so that they can be fixed before it is exploited by hackers. |
| | An Application Programming Interface (API) | An interface that acts as a bridge that allows two applications to interact with each other. For example, you can use CoinGecko's API to fetch the current market price of cryptocurrencies on your website. |
| B | Buy and Hold | This refers to a TokenSets trading strategy which realigns to its target allocation to |

| Index | Term | Description |
|---|---|---|
| | | prevent overexposure to one coin and spreads risk over multiple tokens. |
| | Bonding Curve | A bonding curve is a mathematical curve that defines a dynamic relationship between price and token supply. Bonding curves act as an automated market maker where as the number of supply of a token decreases, the price of the token increases. It is useful as it helps buyers and sellers to access an instant market without the need of intermediaries. |
| C | Cryptocurrency Exchange (Cryptoexchange) | It is a digital exchange that helps users exchange cryptocurrencies. For some exchanges, they also facilitate users to trade fiat currencies to cryptocurrencies. |
| | Custodian | Custodian refers to the third party to have control over your assets. |
| | Fiat-collateralized stablecoin | A stablecoin that is backed by fiat-currency. For example, 1 Tether is pegged to $1. |
| | Crypto-collateralized stablecoin. | A stablecoin that is backed by another cryptocurrency. For example, Dai is backed by Ether at an agreed collateral ratio. |
| | Centralized Exchange (CEX) | Centralized Exchange (CEX) is an exchange that operates in a centralized manner and requires full custody of users' funds. |
| | Collateral | Collateral is an asset you will have to lock-in with the lender in order to borrow another asset. It acts as a guarantor that you will repay your loan. |
| | Collateral Ratio | Collateral ratio refers to the maximum amount of asset that you can borrow after putting collateral into a DeFi decentralized application. |
| | cTokens | cTokens are proof of certificates that you have supplied tokens to Compound's liquidity pool. |
| | Cryptoasset | Cryptoasset refers to digital assets on blockchain. Cryptoassets and cryptocurrencies generally refer to the same |

| Index | Term | Description |
|-------|------|-------------|
| | | thing. |
| | Cover Amount | It refers to the maximum payable money by the insurance company when a claim is made. |
| | Claim Assessment process | It is the obligation by the insurer to review the claim filed by an insurer. After the process, the insurance company will reimburse the money back to the insured based on the Cover Amount. |
| | Composability | Composability is a system design principle that enables applications to be created from component parts. |
| D | Decentralized Finance (DeFi) | DeFi is an ecosystem that allows for the utilization of financial services such as borrowing, lending, trading, getting access to insurance, and more without the need to rely on a centralized entity. |
| | Decentralized Applications (Dapps) | Applications that run on decentralized peer-to-peer networks such as Ethereum. |
| | Decentralized Autonomous Organization (DAO) | Decentralized Autonomous Organizations are rules encoded by smart contracts on the blockchain. The rules and dealings of the DAO are transparent and the DAO is controlled by token holders. |
| | Decentralized Exchange (DEX) | Decentralized Exchange (DEX) allows for trading and direct swapping of tokens without the need to use a centralized exchange. |
| | Derivatives | Derivative comes from the word derive because it is a contract that derives its value from an underlying entity/product. Some of the underlying assets can be commodities, currencies, bonds, or cryptocurrencies. |
| | Dai Saving Rate (DSR) | The Dai Savings Rate (DSR) is an interest earned by holding Dai over time. It also acts as a monetary tool to influence the demand |

| Index | Term | Description |
|---|---|---|
| | | of Dai. |
| | Dashboard | A dashboard is a simple platform that aggregates all your DeFi activities in one place. It is a useful tool to visualize and track where your assets are across the different DeFi protocols. |
| E | Ethereum | Ethereum is an open-source, programmable, decentralized platform built on blockchain technology. Compared to Bitcoin, Ethereum allows for scripting languages which has allowed for application development. |
| | Ether | Ether is the cryptocurrency that powers the Ethereum blockchain. It is the fuel for the apps on the decentralized Ethereum network |
| | ERC-20 | ERC is an abbreviation for Ethereum Request for Comment and 20 is the proposal identifier. It is an official protocol for proposing improvements to the Ethereum network. ERC-20 refers to the commonly adopted standard used to create tokens on Ethereum. |
| | Exposure | Exposure refers to how much you are 'exposed' to the potential risk of losing your investment. For example, price exposure refers to the potential risk you will face in losing your investment when the price moves. |
| F | Future Contract | It is a contract which you enter to buy or sell a particular asset at a certain price at a certain date in the future. |
| | Factory Contract | It is a smart contract that is able to produce other new smart contracts. |
| G | Gas | Gas refers to the unit of measure on the amount of computational effort required to execute a smart contract operation on Ethereum. |
| H | | - |

| Index | Term | Description |
|-------|------|-------------|
| I | IMAP | IMAP stands for Internet Message Access Protocol. It is an Internet protocol that allows email applications to access email on TCP/IP servers. |
| | Index | An index measures the performance of a basket of underlying assets. An index moves when the overall performance of the underlying assets in the basket move. |
| | Inverse | This Synthetix strategy is meant for those who wish to "short" a benchmark. Traders can purchase this when they think a benchmark is due to decrease. |
| J | | - |
| K | Know-Your-Customer (KYC) | Know-Your-Customer (KYC) is a compliance process for business entities to verify and assess their clients. |
| L | Liquidation penalty | It is a fee that a borrower has to pay along with their liquidated collateral when the value of their collateral asset falls below the minimum collateral value. |
| | Liquidity Pools | Liquidity pools are token reserves that sit on smart contracts and are available for users to exchange tokens. Currently the pools are mainly used for swapping, borrowing, lending, and insurance. |
| | Liquidity Risk | A risk when protocols like Compound could run out of liquidity. |
| | Liquidity Providers | Liquidity providers are people who loan their assets into the liquidity pool. The liquidity pool will increase as there are more tokens. |
| | Liquidity Pool Aggregator | It is a system which aggregates liquidity pools from different exchanges and is able to see all available exchange rates in one place. It allows you to compare for the best possible rate. |
| | Leverage | It is an investment strategy to gain higher potential return of the investment by using borrowed money. |

| Index | Term | Description |
|---|---|---|
| M | MakerDAO | MakerDAO is the creator of Maker Platform and DAO stands for Decentralized Autonomous Organisation. MakerDAO's native token is MKR and it is the protocol behind the stablecoins, SAI and DAI. |
| | Market Maker Mechanisms | A Market Maker Mechanism is an algorithm that uses a bonding curve to quote both a buy and a sell price. In the crypto space, Market Maker Mechanism is mainly used by Uniswap or Kyber to swap tokens. |
| | Margin Trading | It is a way of investing by borrowing money from a broker to trade. In DeFi, the borrowing requires you to collateralize assets. |
| | MKR | Maker's governance token. Users can use it to vote for improvement proposal(s) on the Maker Decentralized Autonomous Organization (DAO). |
| | Mint | It refers to the process of issuing new coins/tokens. |
| N | | - |
| O | Order book | It refers to the list of buying and selling orders for a specific asset at various price levels. |
| | Over-collateralization | Over-collateralization refers to the value of collateral asset that must be higher than the value of the borrowed asset. |
| | Option | Option is a right but not the obligation for someone to buy or sell a particular asset at an agreed price on or before an expiry date. |
| P | Price discovery | Price discovery refers to the act of determining the proper price of an asset through several factors such as market demand and supply. |
| | Protocol | A protocol is a base layer of codes that tells something on how to function. For example, Bitcoin and Ethereum blockchains have different protocols. |

| Index | Term | Description |
|-------|------|-------------|
| | Peer-to-Peer | In blockchain, "peer" refers to a computer system or nodes on a decentralized network. Peer-to-Peer (P2P) is a network where each node has an equal permission to validating data and it allows two individuals to interact directly with each other. |
| Q | | - |
| R | Range Bound | This TokenSets strategy automates buying and selling within a designated range and is only intended for bearish or neutral markets. |
| | Rebalance | It is a process of maintaining a desired asset allocation of a portfolio by buying and selling assets in the portfolio. |
| | Risk Assessor | Someone who stakes value against smart contracts in Nexus Mutual. He/she is incentivized to do so to earn rewards in NXM token, as other users buy insurance on the staked smart contracts. |
| S | Smart Contracts | A smart contract is a programmable contract that allows two counterparties to set conditions of a transaction without needing to trust another third party for the execution. |
| | Stablecoins | A stablecoin is a cryptocurrency that is pegged to another stable asset such as the US Dollar. |
| | Spot market | Spot market is the buying and selling of assets with immediate delivery. |
| | Speculative activity | It is an act of buying and selling, while holding an expectation to gain profit. |
| | Stability Fee | It is equivalent to the 'interest rate' which you are required to pay along with the principal debt of the vault. |
| | Slippage | Slippage is the difference between the expected price and the actual price where an order was filled. It is generally caused by low liquidity. |
| | Synths | Synths stand for Synthetic Assets. A Synth is |

| Index | Term | Description |
|-------|------|-------------|
| | | an asset or mixture of assets that has/have the same value or effect as another asset. |
| | Smart Contract Cover | An insurance offer from Nexus Mutal to protect users against hacks in smart contracts that stores value. |
| T | TCP/IP | It stands for Transmission Control Protocol/Internet Protocol. It is a communication protocol to interconnect network devices on the internet. |
| | Total Value Locked | Total Value Locked refers to the cumulative collateral of all DeFi products. |
| | Technical Risk | It refers to the bugs on smart contracts which can be exploited by hackers and cause unintended consequences. |
| | Trading Pairs | A trading pair is a base asset that is paired with its target asset in the trading market. For example, for the ETH/DAI trading pair, the base asset is ETH and its target pair is DAI. |
| | Trend Trading | This strategy uses Technical Analysis indicators to shift from 100% target asset to 100% stable asset based on the implemented strategy. |
| | Tokens | It is a unit of a digital asset. Token often refers to coins that are issued on existing blockchain. |
| | Tokenize | It refers to the process of converting things into digital tradable assets. |
| - | | - |
| V | Value Staked | It refers to how much value the insurer will put up against the target risk. If the value that the insurer staked is lower than the target risk, then it is not coverable. |
| W | Wallet | A wallet is a user-friendly interface to the blockchain network that can be used as a storage, transaction and interaction bridge between the user and the blockchain. |
| X | | - |